Growing your own vegetables

made easy

Which? Books are commissioned and published by Which? Ltd,
2 Marylebone Road, London NW1 4DF
Email: books@which.co.uk

British Library Cataloguing in Publication Data
A catalogue record for this book is available from the British Library

ISBN 978 1 84490 128 9

1 3 5 7 9 10 8 6 4 2

The publishers would like to thank Steve Mercer, Ceri Thomas and Danny Coope for
their help in the preparation of this book.

Consultant editors: Steve Mercer and Ceri Thomas
Project manager: Emma Callery
Designer: Blanche Williams, Harper-Williams Ltd
Proofreader: Sian Stark
Indexer: Chris Bernstein
Printed and bound by Charterhouse, Hatfield
Distributed by Littlehampton Book Services Ltd, Faraday Close, Durrington, Worthing,
West Sussex BN13 3RB

Essential Velvet is an elemental chlorine-free paper produced at Condat in Périgord,
France using timber from sustainably managed forests. The mill is ISO14001 and EMAS
certified.

For a full list of Which? Books, please call 01903 828557, access our
website at www.which.co.uk, or write to Littlehampton Book Services.
For other enquiries call 0800 252 100.

Which?

Growing your own vegetables

made easy

Contents

PLANNING

Grow vegetables in containers	10
Grow vegetables in the border	13
Plan a mini-vegetable plot	17
Allotments	18
Crop rotation	21

PREPARATION & TECHNIQUES

Finding out about your soil	26
Organic matter	29
Prepare the soil	32
Control weeds	35
Control pests	39
Grow vegetables organically	42
Use fertilisers wisely	44
Water sensibly	47
Use space efficiently	51
Sow outdoors	53
Sow indoors	56
Vegetables in the greenhouse	59
Buy plants	61
Frost protection	64

THE PEA FAMILY

Peas	68
Runner beans	72
Dwarf French beans	76
Climbing French beans	80
Broad beans	82

SALAD CROPS

Lettuce	88
Salad leaves	92
Oriental greens	96
Radishes	100
Celery, celeriac and fennel	104
Spinach and chard	108
Cucumbers	111
Asparagus	116

SQUASH

Courgettes, summer squash and marrows	120
Pumpkins and winter squash	125

SUN-LOVING VEGETABLES

Tomatoes	130
Peppers and chillies	135
Aubergines	138
Sweetcorn	141
Artichokes	145

THE CABBAGE FAMILY

Cabbages	150
Cauliflowers	158
Brussels sprouts	162
Calabrese	166
Sprouting broccoli	169
Kale	172
Swedes, turnips and kohl rabi	175

THE ONION FAMILY

Onions and shallots	182
Leeks	187
Spring onions	190
Garlic	191

ROOT CROPS

Potatoes	196
Carrots	202
Beetroot	206
Parsnips	210

RESOURCES

Vegetable calendar	214
Index	220
Credits	224

INTRODUCTION

Growing your own vegetables has become hugely popular in recent years. For many people, taste is at the heart of why they do it as, dissatisfied with cotton-wool tomatoes and tired veg at the supermarket, they want to be sure of eating varieties bred for flavour when they're at their freshest.

Those with children and grandchildren may want to help them understand where their food comes from. Many a passionate gardener started at a young age and getting them interested can bring a lifetime of pleasure. It's wonderful to see how many schools now actively teach gardening to children.

Most of us are keen to spend less money and growing vegetables can be a good way of reducing shopping bills, especially if you can grow early crops and gourmet veg that are expensive in the shops. Freezing and preserving your produce will also keep you well fed, even when there's little growing outdoors.

Finally, for many gardeners, knowing that vegetables haven't been treated with chemicals or flown into their country from miles away makes a big difference in terms of enjoying delicious crops safe in the knowledge that the planet hasn't suffered in their production.

The first chapter explains how to plan your vegetable-growing adventure, whether you want to grow them in containers or on an allotment, while the second chapter focuses on the key techniques you'll need to prepare and look after your plot. Then follow chapters for each group of vegetables, covering preparing the soil, tending to the plants, how to harvest and store, and a handy guide showing exactly what to do each month to produce a healthy crop.

Throughout the book, you'll find gardening tips, step-by-step instructions, and information on keeping pests and diseases at bay. Finally, in the Resources section, we round up the monthly jobs you need to do to keep your plot productive and your harvest plentiful.

Happy growing!

PLANNING

It is still true that if you want to grow a serious amount of produce, a vegetable plot is your best option. But if space in your garden is tight, do not despair. Grow vegetables and herbs in pots on the patio, tucked into flower borders or up fences and trellis. Make a tiny raised bed for a constant supply of fresh salads or a mini-vegetable bed, to grow lots of baby vegetables. It is surprising how much can be fitted into even the smallest garden.

GROW VEGETABLES IN CONTAINERS

Anyone who can grow bedding plants in pots, window boxes or hanging baskets can do equally well with vegetables in containers. You do not even need a garden, just a reasonably sunny place on a windowsill or on your patio. So if your garden has more concrete than soil, you can still grow fresh vegetables.

Some edible plants are attractive in their own right and can hold their own alongside flowering plants. For intense colour, try chard with its brightly coloured stems; red, frilly, loose-leaved lettuce and blue-green kales. For added height, mangetout peas and runner beans will give a good display, as well as a worthwhile crop, in a pot, with some support. If you do not have a greenhouse, tomatoes, especially the dwarf types, are easy in pots or baskets. You could even consider exotic vegetables, such as aubergines or peppers, on a sunny patio.

Some vegetables, while not ornamental, can be grown in large pots to provide useful crops or a tasty treat for a special occasion. Impress your family and friends by serving up new potatoes grown in a large tub or a converted dustbin. Add to that some salad leaves and spring onions, and the occasional courgette or cucumber. Instead of buying baby vegetables, try growing a potful of beetroots, carrots or leeks – an ordinary 30cm pot will equal several supermarket punnets.

How to grow edible plants in containers

Planting one type of vegetable per container seems to work best. Mixed plantings of different vegetables, or vegetables and flowers in the same container, soon lose their visual impact once you start harvesting.

- ❧ You can use almost any container, providing that it is a reasonable size and has drainage holes in the bottom.
- ❧ Where cost is a consideration, use plastic or recycled containers as they are the cheapest. Terracotta looks attractive and is timeless but larger sizes are expensive. The sides of terracotta pots are porous so compost tends to dry out, which can limit cropping of vegetables. Line the inside of the pot with polythene to keep the compost moist.
- ❧ The bigger the container the better, unless you are prepared to water the plants twice a day in summer. As a guide, use at least a 2-litre (15cm) pot for single smaller vegetables – a lettuce, say. Better still, use 10-litre containers (about the size of a domestic bucket) for a single larger vegetable or a group of three or five lettuces. Thirsty crops such as beans, cucumbers and tomatoes will benefit from a 15-litre container (the size of a builder's bucket).
- ❧ Avoid shallow containers that are less than 15cm deep, as these do not give the roots enough depth and, as a result, the compost tends to dry out very quickly.

Which compost?

Multipurpose compost is convenient, and all vegetables will crop well when grown in it, but large quantities can be expensive. Consider using the compost out of growing bags, which should be cheaper; a typical growing bag should contain at least 30 litres of compost.

Tip the contents of the growing bag into deeper containers to make watering easier. You can also reuse compost several times as long as you add slow-release fertiliser each time you replant and don't re-use any from plants that have suffered from vine weevil or disease.

FOR POTS & TUBS

The following vegetables will grow well in pots. You could try others, too, though celery and cauliflowers are likely to bolt. A dwarf red sprout or smaller types of cabbage could be worth trying, but large cabbages and Brussels sprouts will struggle.

Aubergine
Beetroot
Broad beans
Cabbage, spring and summer
Carrots
Chard
Courgettes
French beans (dwarf varieties)
Garlic
Kale
Leeks, baby
Lettuce
Onions/shallots
Oriental greens
Peas, garden and mangetout
Peppers and chillies
Potatoes
Radishes, summer types
Runner beans
Salad leaves
Spinach
Tomatoes

Planting up

1 Mix a spoonful of slow-release fertiliser with the compost and then put into your pots

2 Plant the young plants, firming them down gently as you go. Alternatively sow seeds into the container as you would if you were sowing directly into the soil

3 Cover with 1cm of compost. Leave a 2–3cm gap between the top of the compost and the rim of the pot to make watering easier

Aftercare

Early in the summer, try not to overwater young plants, otherwise the compost will get waterlogged. Once the plants are growing and the weather is warmer, you need to water frequently so the compost never completely dries out.

Some plants, lettuces in particular, start to suffer if left in full sun during the hottest part of the summer. It will be easier to keep them watered if they are in a shaded or semi-shaded part of the patio.

If you haven't added slow-release fertiliser at planting time, you will need to supply extra plant food. Vigorous leafy crops, such as cabbages or lettuces, will need a balanced liquid fertiliser that contains equal proportions of nitrogen, phosphate and potash. For fruiting crops such as cucumbers, peppers and tomatoes, use a liquid tomato feed; this will provide more potash. Follow the application rates for each product.

GROW VEGETABLES IN THE BORDER

It is possible to combine vegetables and flowers imaginatively in the same border to make an attractive feature for your garden. Visually, some vegetables can more than hold their own among flowers. Take the spectacular globe artichoke, feathery asparagus or a pyramid covered in bright-red runner bean flowers, for example.

Most gardens have an ornamental border planted with shrubs and perennials. They are usually in a favourable site with reasonable soil and often have gaps that need filling at various times during the year. They can look very attractive before harvesting.

🌱 Choose vegetable plants with colourful or interesting foliage to set off flowering plants nearby. A patch of early carrots or a group of lettuces, say, will fit in perfectly. Use frilly lettuce, bright-red beetroot or chives as an edible edging.

🌱 Use winter vegetables to brighten up a dull border after the summer flowers have died down. Try the blue-green, strap-shaped leaves of leeks, huge, crinkled Savoy cabbages or forms of kale with red or blue-grey leaves.

🌱 Further back in the border, find room for the larger perennial vegetables, such as globe artichokes.

🌱 Leeks and kale will add winter interest to a border and it is worth leaving a few to flower in the spring.

Although vegetables that run to seed may be a disaster in the vegetable plot, they are not out of place in a border. Bolted lettuces, for example, take on a strange vertical form.

TRY THIS

One way of having a decent-sized vegetable plot, as well as a colourful garden feature, is to create a potager. In a potager, vegetables are grown alongside flowers, herbs and fruit. Beds are arranged in decorative, formal patterns, and separated by paths. The potager could be a simple rustic feature with rectangular beds and firmed earth or bark paths or you can introduce paving to divide up the beds and even raise the beds with edges of board or brick. Try to stick to a simple, symmetrical pattern and use the more ornamental vegetables listed on page 16. Wigwams, obelisks and arches all add vertical interest and impose a sense of symmetry. For a seating area within or to the side of a potager, consider an arbour or a pergola.

TRY THIS

Ensure the supports for climbing plants are in place before planting, as pushing canes and poles into the ground near growing plants can damage their roots. Then tie in the plants to the supports to get them started. Use plant ties or make figure-of-eight ties with garden raffia. Once the plants reach the top of the supports, pinch out their growing tips. Pick the fruits regularly.

How to grow vegetables in your border

Vegetable plants can benefit from the extra shelter provided by a mature, established shrub border early in the season and from the partial shade in high summer. The downside is that they will have to compete for moisture and nutrients with established border plants and may not get enough sunlight.

You will have to abandon the convention for planting vegetables in neat rows. Patches of smaller vegetables or single plants of larger ones will look more natural in a border. Follow the cottage garden approach of just filling any available space with whatever vegetable or herb takes your fancy.

To give your vegetables a decent start in a border:

1 Fork the area over with a garden fork to loosen the soil, clearing the area of perennial weeds as you work. Work in some well-rotted organic matter and add a scattering of balanced fertiliser

2 Then water the area thoroughly before sowing or planting the vegetables. If you are putting plants into your border, use a trowel rather than a garden spade to dig the holes

3 Mulch larger plants such as courgettes and bush tomatoes to keep the soil underneath moist and to prevent weeds from growing

4 Vigorous leafy plants will benefit from a top-up of a nitrogen feed in summer (see page 44)

5 Be vigilant about monitoring for pests, such as cabbage white butterflies and aphids. Natural predators, such as birds and ladybirds, should keep most pests under control except for slugs and snails. You may need to take some precautions against these (see pages 40–1)

Long-term plants

Perennial vegetables are worth growing in a border as they can be tricky to accommodate in a small vegetable plot where annual crop rotation is practised.

🌱 Globe artichokes look spectacular in leaf and flower. They are large plants, so put them towards the back of the border. Give them plenty of room and generous amounts of organic matter.

🌱 The feathery foliage of asparagus provides a backdrop for large border flowers.

Annual fillers

Treat summer vegetables just as you would bedding plants. Start the tender types off in small pots somewhere warm and stand them in a sheltered spot. Plant them with a trowel, using the spacings given in this book. An easy alternative to sowing seed if you need only a few plants is to buy small plants from the garden centre (see page 61).

Winter fillers

Borders that are planted with tender summer bedding have gaps over the dormant season – from late autumn to late spring. Winter or early summer vegetables such as kale or broad beans can be planted late in the autumn and will occupy the space before the herbaceous plants have emerged and before the summer bedding is planted.

If you can find the space in mid- to late summer, add a few hardy winter vegetables such as leeks, Savoy cabbages and kales. If you have not raised your own from seed, buy young plants and plant them where summer annuals will be cleared in autumn. Give them a good start by adding a little general fertiliser when you plant them.

Vegetable climbers

If you are short of space, grow vertically – many vegetables make attractive climbers. Runner beans were first grown as colourful ornamental climbers rather than for their beans. The tall pea variety 'Carouby de Maussane' is often mistaken for a sweet pea, and trailing marrows and smaller squash varieties look wonderful as the ripe fruits hang down from arches and pergolas.

Growing vegetable climbers in an ornamental garden rather than a vegetable plot has a couple of advantages:

- The climbers can be sited where they will not cast shade over other edible crops.
- Permanent existing supports such as walls, fences and trellis can be used instead of temporary supports.

The most useful permanent supports are south-facing. Look around your garden for possible sites:

- House walls, sheds, garage walls and tall boundary fences could all be candidates for support.
- If there is no soil to plant into, use large tubs filled with compost (see pages 11–12). A wall or fence will need horizontal wires, netting or trellis panels fitted to support the climbers.
- In the open garden, a row of runner beans trained up bamboo canes or hazel poles could be used as a garden divider.

FOR BORDERS

Artichoke, globe
Asparagus
Beetroot
Broad, French, runner beans
Cabbage, winter
Carrots
Courgettes/ marrows
Fennel
Kale
Leeks
Lettuce
Onions, salad
Oriental greens
Peppers/chillies
Pumpkins/squash
Spinach and chard
Sweetcorn
Tomatoes

PLAN A MINI-VEGETABLE PLOT

In a small garden, you will not have room for a conventional vegetable plot. Instead, you could have a mini-vegetable plot full of baby vegetables. Baby vegetables are often preferred for their appearance and tenderness, and if you buy them from a supermarket, they are more expensive than normal-sized vegetables.

You will be surprised at how much you can fit into a mini-vegetable plot: rows of root vegetables are just 15cm apart, and leafy crops such as cabbages, cauliflowers and lettuces are just 15cm apart each way. Baby vegetables can be grown in the following three ways:

Pick conventional varieties while they are young. This works for root crops such as beetroot, carrots (use an early variety), leeks and parsnips.

Grow dwarf varieties, for example of cabbages and lettuces, which will not grow larger even if allowed more space.

Grow vegetables at closer spacings than normal. This technique works well for baby cauliflowers, calabrese and all types of cabbage.

Although these techniques will work with most varieties, it is worth looking for varieties sold specifically for mini-vegetable production. Often, a combination of all three techniques works best:

🌱 Start with a suitable variety
🌱 Grow it at a close spacing
🌱 Harvest when young and tender.

Other vegetables, such as courgettes and dwarf French beans, are picked small and sold as baby vegetables, but the plants take up as much space as conventional varieties. Cucumbers with naturally small fruit and cherry tomatoes also grow on normal-sized plants.

TRY THIS
To make your mini-vegetable bed neater, consider edging it with boards or use a raised-bed kit. This will raise it above the surrounding garden, and enable you to improve the soil by adding organic matter and cut down on watering.

FOR BABY VEGETABLES
Beetroot
Cabbage
Calabrese
Carrots
Cauliflower
Leeks
Lettuce
Onions
Parsnips

planning

17

ALLOTMENTS

You do not even need a garden to grow vegetables – you can rent an allotment. If you are new to vegetable growing, you can rely on plenty of friendly advice and support too from a community of fellow gardeners.

TIP

If you have a choice of plots, go for one that has been cultivated recently – breaking in an overgrown plot is a tough job (but see page 20).

Choosing an allotment

Find out about the allotment sites in your area. Some are run privately by a committee of allotment holders, while others are run by the local council. Rent and the facilities provided vary from area to area. A thriving site could have purpose-built sheds for each plot, a trading hut for cheap gardening sundries and even a clubhouse.

Waiting lists Many areas are experiencing high demand for allotments and you may have to go onto a waiting list for several years before you get your plot. Most sites release plots in the autumn after doing their annual inspection of how well cared for the plots are.

Talk to allotment holders before you agree to rent a plot:

- Ask about the security of the site – vandalism and petty theft can be a problem on some allotments.
- Find out what the major pests are. Some sites have a problem with rabbits, which are hard to control.
- A whole plot is normally about 250 sq m – a large area to dig over in one go. Find out if you can rent a half- or quarter-plot to get started; you can always take on more later.

- Check that there is a tap nearby and that access is easy for bulky deliveries such as compost.
- Try to find out, from neighbouring plot-holders, about the recent history of your particular plot. For example, did the previous owner dig in lots of organic matter, use fertilisers and pesticides excessively, or practise crop rotation. Does the site have a history of problem diseases such as clubroot on brassicas or white rot on onions?

Getting started

Getting off to a good start with an allotment can make all the difference. The best time to start is in the autumn or winter, as this will give you plenty of time to plan and get the soil right.

If the plot has been cultivated recently, it is worthwhile clearing any crop remains and digging it over roughly, removing any perennial weeds you come across. On heavy soils, aim to rough-dig before midwinter and leave the frost to create a crumbly soil structure. On lighter soils, you can get away with digging in late winter.

Aim to work in a generous amount of well-rotted organic matter – a barrow-load to every 2 sq m should be plenty. Someone on the allotment site will be able to tell you where to get local supplies of bulky organic matter – farmyard or stable manure, or mushroom compost. The aim should be to have the whole plot ready to start sowing and planting by early spring.

An overgrown plot

You may have no choice but to take on a plot that has been left uncultivated for several years. This is a daunting prospect but the secret is to break down the task into manageable chunks.

- Take a small area and clear it thoroughly, rather than trying to tackle the whole plot at once.
- If necessary, remove any undergrowth with a petrol trimmer – these can be hired, along with protective clothing, by the day from a DIY hire shop.
- Cover any ground you cannot clear immediately with black plastic weighed down with large stones, or else use old carpet. This will weaken and eventually kill even perennial weeds. (See pages 35–7 for more information on weed control.)

Your fellow plot-holders will be only too pleased that you are tackling an overgrown plot, so most will be more than happy to pass on their expertise and opinions. But do not be afraid to break with the traditional approach, for example, by building a couple of raised beds, and remember to grow what you and your family want to eat, not simply what everyone else is growing.

CROP ROTATION

Wherever you plant your vegetables, crop rotation is essential. This means growing certain crops on a different area of land each year in a three- or four-year cycle. There are many benefits to this system.

🌱 Moving the crops around helps to prevent some troublesome soil pests and diseases from building up to damaging levels.

🌱 By swapping the main groups of vegetables around in a regular order you can make the most efficient use of the nutrients in the soil because different types of crops require different amounts of nutrients.

Anyone who wants to grow crops with the minimum amount of chemicals and fertilisers should practise crop rotation. The amount of organic matter available is often limited, so you need to make sure it goes to the hungriest crops. In a crop-rotation scheme, you need only apply the manure to a third of the area in any one year.

It is also convenient to grow related crops together, so that, for example, members of the cabbage family can be protected from the insect pests that attack them all. Likewise, green vegetables that require regular watering can be separated from root crops, which will survive without watering.

Smaller vegetable plots

On small vegetable plots, conventional crop rotation is not practical, so instead aim to separate the main crop groupings as far as possible. At the very least, try to grow vegetables such as potatoes, onions and the cabbage family, which are prone to soil pests and diseases, on a different area each year and fit any other crops around them. You do not need to follow a strict rotation, but keep a record each year and try to ensure that key crops do not go on the same bed for at least another three years.

Vegetable families

Here is a summary of the main members of each family, the problems that can be prevented by crop rotation and the care requirements they have in common.

Cabbage family

Vegetables Broccoli, Brussels sprouts, cabbages, calabrese, cauliflowers, Chinese cabbage and other oriental greens, kale and radishes.
Potential problems Clubroot; pests such as cabbage aphid, flea beetle, cabbage root fly, cabbage caterpillars can be kept at bay with fine mesh; rabbit netting and pigeon netting may also be needed for over winter crops.
Requirements Alkaline soil – lime if acid (see page 27); soil that was manured for a previous crop; a large amount of fertiliser (see pages 44–6).

Onion family

Vegetables All types of onions, chives, garlic, leeks and shallots.
Potential problems Eelworm and white rot; leek rust cannot be controlled by rotation.
Requirements Soil that has been manured for a previous crop needs only a small amount of fertiliser (see pages 44–6); does not generally need watering.

Pea family

Vegetables Garden and mangetout peas, broad beans, French and runner beans.
Potential problems Various root rots.
Requirements Organic matter, such as manure, but little fertiliser.

Potato family

Vegetables Potatoes and tomatoes, also aubergines and peppers.
Potential problems Eelworm, powdery scab (but not common scab); potato blight.

Requirements No lime needed, moderate amounts of fertiliser, organic matter if it can be spared; all require protection from late spring frosts and may need spraying to prevent blight.

Root crops
Vegetables Carrots, parsley and parsnips.
Potential problems Various root rots, including parsnip canker; carrot fly can be prevented with a physical barrier of garden fleece or fine netting.

Other crops
These are not related to the main groups above and can be fitted anywhere in the rotation.
Beetroot, chard and leaf beet and spinach Need fertiliser but not organic matter.
Celery and celeriac Need a rich, moisture-retentive soil, with plenty of manure and regular watering.
Lettuces Need organic matter, nitrogen fertiliser and regular watering; they are often grown with cabbage family crops.
Marrows, courgettes, cucumbers, pumpkins and squash Benefit from a moisture-retentive soil and can be grown on any well-manured area or on manure-filled planting holes.
Sweetcorn Generally not fussy about soil but is sensitive to frost, so should be planted late, when it can usefully follow early peas or beans.
Perennial vegetables such as asparagus Best kept out of beds used for crop rotation. Grow them in their own bed on the plot.

Larger vegetable plots
If you can, divide your plot into four rotation groups with root vegetables and onions making up Plot D.

THREE-YEAR ROTATION

YEAR 1	YEAR 2	YEAR 3
Plot A Root vegetables	**Plot A** Pea and onion families	**Plot A** Cabbage family
Plot B Pea and onion families	**Plot B** Cabbage family	**Plot B** Root vegetables
Plot C Cabbage family	**Plot C** Root vegetables	**Plot C** Pea and onion families

PREPARATION & TECHNIQUES

Whether you are new to growing your own vegetables or have been doing it for years, it pays to know the techniques that really produce results so that you can get the most from your plot. In this chapter you will find advice ranging from making the most of your soil and controlling weeds and pests to buying plants and avoiding problems with frost. So go on, start digging.

Dig a hole 45cm square and 45cm deep in late winter. Fill it halfway up with water and put on a waterproof cover. Check the level of water in the hole after an hour and again the next day. If the water has disappeared within an hour, it is free-draining soil, but if it is still there the next day, the soil is wet or waterlogged.

FINDING OUT ABOUT YOUR SOIL

While almost all soils can be improved to make them suitable for growing vegetables, you need to know what type of soil you have to start with.

Texture

To find out more about your soil, simply dig a couple of holes in the ground and look at the soil that comes up. Are there a lot of stones or lumps of chalk? Is it baked rock hard? Or is it like dust?

🌱 Take up a handful of soil from 10–15cm down. Squeeze the soil: if it feels spongy, a bit like compost, it has a high organic content.

🌱 Rub some soil between your fingertips – a gritty texture indicates that sand is present, while a smooth texture points to a loam or clay soil.

🌱 Knead the soil in your hands – can you work it into a ball? A soil that cannot be moulded in this way and keeps breaking up contains very few clay particles.

The ideal gardening soil is loam, which is a mixture of sand and clay particles. It can hold moisture in summer, yet water can drain through in winter. Where there is a high proportion of clay, you can have problems with waterlogging. Try rolling the ball of soil into a sausage shape, then bending it into a circle in your hand; a loam does not have enough clay to make a circle but a soil rich in clay does.

Acid or alkaline?

A simple pH test that you can do yourself will tell you within a couple of minutes whether your soil is acid or alkaline. Soil tests are done in test tubes so the samples tested are a tiny proportion of the total soil you want to know about. For that reason, it is vital to get a soil sample that is accurately representative. Large areas are best divided into sections, which are individually tested:

 Lay out four bamboo canes in a W-shape across the area

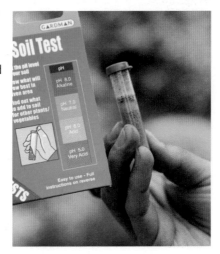

 Using a clean trowel, dig down to about 15cm. Take out some soil at the end of each cane (five samples in total)

TRY THIS
Acid soils can be corrected by adding ground limestone. The amount you add depends on the soil type and the initial pH. Add the lime to the soil in autumn and wait until spring before applying manure or fertiliser. Nitrogen can be lost if lime is applied at the same time as manures and fertilisers.

3 Remove stones, weed and roots and then mix the five portions together in a clean bucket. Take out the amount needed for the test (usually 500g for a full analysis)

 Take a half-teaspoon of soil and drop it into the test tube of chemical supplied. Add water and shake well

5 Check the colour of the liquid against the colour chart supplied. On the pH scale, 7.0 is neutral, a higher figure is alkaline and a lower one acid. Most vegetables prefer a pH within the range pH 6.5–7.5, with brassicas preferring the upper end

You should test the pH of your garden soil every two to three years.

Growing vegetables on different soils

Stony Use a garden fork to loosen the soil and put a lot of organic matter on the soil, rather than trying to dig down with a spade.

Chalk Add lots of organic matter to improve the moisture-holding capacity of the soil; then feed from spring to summer. Early sowings should do well.

Sandy These soils are often acid, so may need liming regularly (see 'Try this' on page 27). They are also free draining, so add plenty of organic matter. Spent mushroom compost is a good choice because it has a neutral pH. Water, mulch and feed from spring to summer. Early sowings thrive.

Loam This is ideal soil for vegetables, but it may need lime, depending on the results of a pH test. It is still worth adding some organic matter but fertiliser is less vital.

Clay This is a fertile soil but it can become waterlogged and be slow to warm up in spring. Start plants off in pots of compost, use cloches to warm the soil and make raised beds. Digging will aerate the soil, but keep off the ground when it is wet and sticky or it will quickly become compacted. The best time to dig is either in late autumn before winter rains or as the soil is drying in spring. Organic matter will help to open up the soil but fertiliser may not be necessary.

ORGANIC MATTER

All soils benefit from organic matter, the only exception being peaty soils, which are rare in the UK. Well-rotted organic matter is a catch-all phrase for a number of materials of plant or animal origin that have been composted down to make a bulky soil improver. It improves the structure of soils that are waterlogged, compacted or too free draining and feeds a hidden army of soil creatures and organisms that all contribute to the general health and fertility of the soil.

Unlike fertilisers, organic matter is added by the fork or barrow-load rather than being sprinkled on. As it is used up by the soil creatures, regular applications are needed.

Garden compost

Recycle as much organic matter as you can from your own garden and kitchen by turning it into garden compost. Collect all the material together in a bin, choosing from one of the following:

Ready-made bins The best types are large plastic cylinders or cones with a lid. Make the compost in batches, then lift the bin off, leaving a composted heap that can be covered until it is used. Then start filling the bin again.

DIY bins The ideal size for an effective compost bin is about 1 cubic m. If you have room, make two side by side so you can turn compost from one bin to another to get air into the mixture.

Site the bin in a shaded area out of view but with access for a wheelbarrow. It should be on free-draining earth (not on concrete or paving) so that worms and insects can migrate in and help aerate the compost. If the soil is wet, put down a layer of twigs first. Leave gaps at the bottom of the sides for ventilation. You are now ready to make your own compost.

1 Fill the bin with a mixture of woody material and green material

2 You can add a handful of nitrogen fertiliser or a shovel full of garden compost or garden soil to get the process going but do not bother with special compost activators

3 Keep the contents damp but not sodden. A square of old carpet or sacking on the top will hold in moisture and warmth

4 Add a waterproof cover to keep heavy rain off

TIP
To speed things up for leaf mould, shred the leaves by running a mower over them before storing them.

Left unturned, the heap will take about a year to become dark and crumbly and ready to use. However, it can take as little as ten weeks if you turn your heap every week.

Leaf mould

Rather than putting piles of autumn leaves in the compost bin, stack them in their own wire enclosure to rot down into leaf moyld. They do not need warmth or a cover as the leaves are broken down by fungi rather than bacteria (as is the case with compost). Just water the leaves now and again, and in a couple of years the leaves will have rotted down. If you want leaf moyld in as little as 12 months, shred the leaves by running over them with a lawnmower beforehand.

Other sources

Most gardeners need more organic matter than they can make in their own gardens. Commercial products usually sold as soil improvers in 80-litre bags are ready processed and adequate for improving the soil of a small border or raised bed. For a larger area, you need a loose load of manure or spent mushroom compost. Municipal compost or green waste is available cheaply in some areas.

Well-rotted manure can be used straight away, but if it is fresh you will need to compost it. Make a heap and water it if it is dry. Cover it with a sheet of plastic secured at the edges; this will prevent nutrients being washed out. In about six months it will be ready for use. Horse or cow manure is preferable. Poultry manure is best regarded as a fertiliser (see pages 44–6).

Spent mushroom compost is a mixture of horse manure or specially treated straw, peat and lime, which is used to grow mushrooms commercially. After harvesting, it is sold off. It is an ideal soil improver because it is not as acid as other manures. Stack it under cover to allow chemical steriliants to break down.

WHAT TO PUT IN YOUR COMPOST BIN

Fruit and vegetable waste, including tea bags and coffee grounds
Pet litter, from hamsters and rabbits for example
Shredded newspaper and corrugated cardboard (both in moderation)
Grass clippings and green prunings
Remains of bedding plants, top growth from perennials and used compost from containers
Woody prunings only if shredded first

DO NOT ADD
Cat litter
Cooked food waste
Perennial weeds
Annual weeds in flower
Diseased or virus-infected plants

preparation & techniques

PREPARE THE SOIL

Digging is the traditional method for clearing a vegetable plot at the end of the season and preparing it for the next. But organic gardeners question the need for annual digging, pointing out that it destroys the soil's natural structure and can bring a fresh crop of weed seeds to the surface. Digging is also often impractical when growing vegetables among other plants. Whether you dig every year, every few years or not at all depends on where you are growing your vegetables and on the underlying soil (see pages 26–8).

Breaking new ground

When starting off a new vegetable plot or constructing raised vegetable beds, it is advisable to prepare the ground thoroughly. Digging breaks up compacted soil, improving drainage and aeration. At the same time, you can remove perennial weed roots and incorporate bulky organic matter.

It is worth doing a thorough job. First dig a hole at least 45cm deep. If there is a hard layer below the surface that could impede drainage, this should be broken up by double digging (see opposite). If the soil is fairly loose and free draining, single digging should suffice.

Double digging

1 Dig a trench about 30cm wide and to the depth of the spade. You should only move the topsoil, not the underlying subsoil. Barrow the soil from this first trench to the other end of the area being dug

2 Spread a layer of well-rotted manure in the trench and, using a garden fork, dig over the bottom of the trench to the depth of the fork. Break up any hard layer, loosen the subsoil and mix in the manure

3 Dig a second trench parallel to the first. But this time throw the topsoil forward to fill in the first trench, then repeat Step 2

4 Repeat this procedure across the whole area, until you are left with a final trench. After completing step 2 for the final trench, use the soil from the first trench to top it up

Single digging

Follow Steps 1, 3 and 4 above but not step 2. If you want to incorporate manure into the ground at the same time, spread it on the surface so that it is mixed into the topsoil as you dig.

TIP
To look after your back, warm up properly first and spread the digging over several sessions.

Annual digging

Some gardeners still prefer to dig over the vegetable plot each winter.

On a heavy clay soil, aim to complete digging by Christmas. Try to invert each lump of soil to bury annual weeds, but leave the clods intact. The action of frost and rain will break down the clods to leave a crumbly soil by spring.

On light, sandy soils, wait until spring before digging. Often a hard crust forms on the surface over winter and this needs to be broken up before sowing or planting.

Mulching

It is better to add organic matter as a surface mulch in the spring, so the nutrients benefit your crops. Spread organic matter on the surface of the soil in a deep layer, preferably at least 5cm thick. It will prevent weed seeds germinating and help to retain moisture within the soil. In time, earthworms will drag the mulch down into the soil, so you do not need to dig it in. You will need to reapply mulch every spring. Mulching cannot tackle underlying problems such as compaction, but it will help to maintain a well-structured and fertile soil.

Trenching

Preparing a trench can help in two ways. It can increase the moisture retention of the part of the vegetable plot where runner beans or other moisture-sensitive crops are to grow. It is also a convenient way to dispose of tough crop remains that are slow to rot down in the compost heap. Dig a trench about 60cm wide and 30cm deep in the autumn. Fill it over winter with crop debris, manure and old growing-bag compost and gradually replace the topsoil. Leave it to settle before planting in spring.

Planting holes

The same principal as trenching applies, but on a smaller scale. Dig a hole about 30cm deep and 30cm across for one plant, such as a courgette, and incorporate plenty of organic matter into the soil at the bottom of the hole before refilling with soil. This is useful when planting moisture-sensitive crops into an established border.

CONTROL WEEDS

Weeds compete with your plants for moisture and nutrients so you need to control them promptly, otherwise crop yield will be adversely affected. Some weeds can also harbour pests that then move on to growing crops.

Tackling a large, neglected plot full of perennial weeds such as a disused allotment is very hard work, and you may want to use a weedkiller containing glyphosate to get a head start even if you plan to grow vegetables organically eventually. Once the cultivated ground is more or less weed-free, it can be kept that way without using chemicals at all.

Clearing weedy ground

When perennial weeds have got the upper hand, it is an uphill struggle to get rid of them. Even though you may have dealt with the top growth, the plants may regrow from tiny fragments of roots or stems left in the ground. A petrol rotovator can make the problem worse by cutting up the roots and spreading them around the plot. There are three recommended ways of clearing weed-infested ground.

Covering Cut back the top growth of the weeds, then cover the ground with black polythene sheeting or old carpet. Provided the cover is kept in place for at least a year, the weeds will die. This is the easiest way to clear a plot if you can afford to wait a year.

Spraying A quick method is to use a systemic weedkiller containing glyphosate to kill weeds. This travels down to the roots and kills the weeds within a few weeks. You may need to apply the weedkiller more than once if the weeds re-grow. Glyphosate breaks down rapidly on contact with the soil so you will be able to plant within weeks. The ideal time to do this is in late spring to early summer, when the weeds are growing rapidly. Take care to avoid spray drifting on to other plants.

Digging The traditional method of clearing a new vegetable plot is to dig it over and remove every piece of perennial weed root by hand. It is very time-consuming but if done thoroughly should remove most perennial weeds. Deep-rooting weeds such as bindweed will need persistent removal over several years.

Keeping beds weed-free

Once you have cleared the beds of perennial weeds, you will still need to be vigilant. Annual weeds produce seed in vast quantities, and these lie dormant in the soil for many years. Cultivating the soil by digging will bring weed seeds to the surface, where they will germinate, grow and set more seed. Some annual weeds, such as chickweed, flower and set seed remarkably quickly, so it is vital to control them promptly. You can keep weeds down in several ways.

Loose mulches prevent light reaching weed seeds and triggering germination. Cover the soil surface with a 5cm-layer of loose mulch, such as weed-free garden compost; well-rotted farmyard manure or composted green waste. For an ornamental border, chipped bark or cocoa shells are attractive but rather expensive.

A sheet mulch, such as woven polypropylene or black plastic (make holes with a garden fork to prevent rain collecting in puddles) is laid over the soil and the edges secured. Sheet mulches are effective at keeping paths between beds weed-free in the long term. Use them on their own or under paving or gravel. Widely spaced crops such as courgettes, sweetcorn and potatoes can be grown through sheet mulch – cut a cross in the sheet, fold back the four triangular flaps, dig a hole and plant.

TRY THIS
A quick way to get rid of annual weeds before sowing or planting is to prepare the seedbed and cover it with a cloche or sheet of clear plastic. Weeds will germinate within a couple of weeks and can be hoed off.

Hoeing is particularly useful for closely-spaced vegetables where mulching is not practical. Use a Dutch hoe for weeding between rows or a swoe (this has a blade shaped like an elongated golf club) among wider-spaced vegetables. Keep the blade sharp so it skims along the surface of the soil, severing the weeds. The most effective time to hoe is early in the morning on a hot, dry day, when the hoed weeds will quickly shrivel up.

Top five weeds to look out for

Weeds grow faster as the weather warms up. Dandelion (1), bindweed (2), hairy bittercress (3), fat hen (4) and chickweed (5) are worth dealing with promptly before they take hold. Weed beds and pots little and often, and hoe weed seedlings on dry, sunny days so they shrivel and die and don't re-root. For problem weeds such as couch grass, you'll have to dig down with a trowel or hand fork and follow their spreading roots, teasing out as much as you can.

CONTROL PESTS

The pleasure of growing your own produce can be short-lived if slugs or rabbits get to your crops before you do, and greenfly on a salad is rarely appetising. However, not every crop gets ravaged by pests and diseases each year. In most cases, using barriers to prevent pests reaching the crop, and keeping an eye on plants so you can tackle pest or disease outbreaks early on, are the only regular steps you need to take.

Erect barriers

Early in the year, a layer of garden fleece will protect young plants from flying insects such as aphids, carrot fly and cabbage white butterflies. Later, in the summer, crops under fleece can scorch, so use very fine plastic netting instead. Drape them over hoops of stiff wire to give the crop room to grow. Weigh down or secure the edges so pests cannot get in.

If your garden suffers from pigeons or rabbits, use pigeon netting draped over supports to protect overwintering crops. Rabbits can be kept out by installing a barrier of chicken wire fencing 1m high above ground and buried 30cm below the surface.

Use pesticides

Pesticide is a term used to cover a number of products including fungicides that deal with diseases, and insecticides that combat insect pests. As long as you follow the instructions, they are safe to use. Pay particular attention to the dilution rate, note which pest or disease they are recommended for and follow any advice on how long to wait before harvesting after spraying. Note that some pesticides are not suitable for edible crops or particular plants. Spray in the evening if possible to avoid harming pollinating insects.

You can buy pesticides in a ready-to-use form such as a spray gun. These are convenient to use but can work out expensive for a vegetable plot. Buying a concentrate that you dilute and apply with a pressure sprayer is more economical. Some insecticides are applied as a dust.

Organic gardeners prefer not to use pesticides at all, although some are used as a last resort (see page 43).

Slugs and snails

A combination of vigilance and timely control methods should help to keep young crops safe from slugs and snails. Attacks are worse in the mild, damp periods of spring and autumn, and seedlings and young leafy crops are most vulnerable.

🌱 Slug pellets are a popular control method as they are cheap and easy to apply. Organic pellets based on ferric phosphate are as effective as chemical ones based on metaldehyde. Scatter the pellets sparingly around the plants and re-apply after two weeks, sooner if it rains. For anyone with a sizeable vegetable plot, the low cost of pellets compared with other treatments is persuasive.

- A biological control based on nematode worms is effective for six weeks against slugs if applied before planting.
- Young plants can be protected from surface slugs with rings cut from plastic bottles. Cut sections 10cm high and push them 2–3cm into the ground.
- Copper tape is worth trying around containers or small raised beds.
- An entirely organic method is to visit the vegetable plot at night with a torch. Collect any slugs and snails you spot; repeat the visits several times to reduce the slug and snail population. Alternatively, start plants in small pots or modular trays and plant them out when they are large enough to survive.

Aphids: especially greenfly and blackfly

Greenfly and blackfly are just a couple of the 500 or so aphids found in gardens. All aphids breed prodigiously and suck the sap from plants. Plants are weakened, and the yield can be affected. In addition, some aphids spread viruses from one plant to another, for example, mosaic virus can be introduced into a courgette plant, with fatal results. Their excretion will make the leaves sticky, too, and encourage a black sooty mould. Treat as soon as the flies appear and repeat if necessary.

- Insecticides based on soft soap or pyrethrum kill aphids on contact. Others work by being absorbed into the plant sap and killing aphids that feed on the sap. Apply them in the evening to avoid harming bees.
- Alternatively, rely on natural predators such as birds and insects to eat aphids; use a crop cover; nip out any badly infested plants, or rub them off as you see them.

Controlling diseases

With the exception of potato blight and clubroot, which can be prevented by pre-emptive fungicide sprays or liming, respectively, the gardener's options are limited. Vigilance, combined with scrupulous hygiene and good husbandry, will help. Advice on specific problems can be found in most entries in the relevant chapters in this book.

GROW VEGETABLES ORGANICALLY

One of the best reasons for growing your own vegetables is that you can be absolutely sure how they have been grown and what has been sprayed on them. The aim of organic gardening is to work with nature, rather than trying to control it. So relying on natural predators to keep down pests plays a large part. Anything you can do to encourage a wide range of wildlife into the garden – by creating favourable habitats such as ponds, meadows and hedgerows, for example – will make it more likely that natural predators will help to control pests on your vegetables.

Feeding the soil

Organic gardeners aim to build up soil fertility over the long term, rather than supplying soluble man-made nutrients directly to plants. In practice, this means adding plenty of organic matter and caring for the soil in the ways outlined on pages 32–4. In addition, you might want to consider where manures have come from: for example, an organic farm rather than a conventional one.

It is now recommended that more care is taken over the amount of manure applied: no more than about one barrow-load of manure or two barrow-loads of garden compost to 10 sq m of ground each year. If you follow a crop-rotation system (see pages 21–3), apply manure to the crops that benefit most.

Pest and disease control

There are many organic ways to prevent damage by pests or diseases:

- Crop rotation (see pages 21–3).
- Physical barriers such as fine-mesh netting and sections of plastic drink bottles (see pages 39 and 41).
- Sowings timed to miss the most vulnerable period.
- Hand-picking larger pests such as slugs, snails and caterpillars.
- Encouraging insect predators such as ladybirds, lacewings and hoverflies, ground beetles, hedgehogs and birds, which will eat aphids or other pests.
- In the greenhouse, biological control is an effective alternative to chemicals (see below).

Acceptable pesticides

Generally, organic gardeners do not use pesticides, but some based on naturally occurring substances can be used as a last resort. Bordeaux mixture can be used to prevent potato blight. Insecticides based on soft soap, plant fatty acids and pyrethrum are all acceptable. Although these products are derived from natural materials, they will also kill beneficial insects, so should be used with care – in the evening when bees are not active, for example.

5 MINUTE JOB

Control whitefly and other flying pests in the greenhouse with yellow sticky traps. Hang them on wires near your plants for chemical-free insect control.

Biological control in the greenhouse

This is quite expensive and involves introducing natural predators as soon as the first signs of the pest are seen. The controls are available from mail-order suppliers and follow the suppliers' instructions for the temperature of the greenhouse and other special requirements. For:

- Red spider mites, use phytoseiulus
- Vine weevil, use parasitic nematodes
- Whitefly, use a tiny wasp called encarsia

USE FERTILISERS WISELY

Vegetables grow fast compared with many other plants and need a readily available supply of nutrients while they are growing. Garden soil contains most of the essential minerals that plants need for growth, but the following three major nutrients are needed in relatively large quantities.

Nitrogen makes plant proteins including chlorophyll, which gives plants their green colour. Lack of nitrogen slows growth and yellows the leaves; later, the stems may be an unnatural red or purple. The nitrogen used by plants is in a soluble form (nitrates or ammonium

salts) so it is easily washed out of the soil during heavy rain. Free-draining soils such as sandy or chalky soils are most likely to leave plants short of nitrogen.

Phosphorus is important for growth and respiration. It is needed in the form of soluble phosphates for the formation of plant organs such as roots.

Potassium, in the form of potash, acts as a regulator in plant cells and also affects the size and quality of flowers and fruits.

Both phosphorus and potassium are usually present in sufficient quantities in garden soils.

Magnesium This is the only other nutrient to worry about. Lack of this minor nutrient shows up as yellowing between the veins on leaves of tomatoes, especially growing in containers. Look for a tomato feed which includes magnesium or water with a solution of Epsom salts (about 200g to 10 litres of water).

Sources of nutrients

Organic matter added to improve the structure of the soil will also contribute to soil fertility. However, the quantities of nutrients present in organic matter is variable. Manure contains a reasonable amount of nitrogen; 1kg of cow or horse manure could contribute as much nitrogen as 25g of growmore. On the other hand, leaf mould and bark chips contribute very little useable nutrient, and woodchips can actually remove nitrogen from the soil.

If you do need to add potash or phosphate, choose between the naturally occurring rock potash or bonemeal, which are acceptable to organic gardeners, or the man-made sulphate of potash or superphosphate.

The organic approach is to feed the soil with organic matter rather than rely on fertilisers. If your soil is low in nutrients and you cannot add sufficient organic matter, fertilisers offer a quick and easy way to supply your plants' needs. It is important to supply sufficient fertilisers for heavy feeders, such as brassicas and maincrop potatoes (those that are ready between July and October), but not too much as nutrients can be washed out of the soil by rain and contribute to pollution.

Types of fertiliser

Balanced or general fertilisers contain more or less equal amounts of nitrogen, phosphate and potash. Examples of widely used balanced fertilisers include growmore and blood, fish and bone.

Straight fertilisers add just one nutrient, so, if your soil has plenty of phosphorus and potash, you can top up the nitrogen level annually by applying sulphate of ammonia or nitrochalk. Both of these add 21 per cent nitrogen, but nitrochalk is more useful for vegetable growing as it contains lime and so does not lower the soil pH.

Liquid feeds or fertilisers containing seaweed extract are a good source of all the other minor elements.

Organic fertilisers are derived from plants or animals. Balanced fertilisers you may come across are pelleted chicken manure and blood, fish and bone (this often has extra potash added). Organic straight nitrogen fertilisers are dried blood or hoof and horn, both with 13 per cent nitrogen.

Applying fertiliser

Most fertilisers are sold as powders or granules. Rather than apply all the fertiliser to the growing vegetable in one go, spread the dose throughout the growing season. Typically, about half the amount is raked or forked into the soil before sowing or planting. The rest is then applied when the crop is halfway to maturity.

Liquid feeds are essential for crops growing in containers or for getting nutrients to plants quickly. Liquid feeds for leafy crops are balanced, such as liquid growmore, but the most widely sold liquid fertiliser is tomato feed, which is high in potash to encourage fruit production.

To apply the fertiliser, always follow the instructions on the packaging.

WATER SENSIBLY

Some vegetables can crop even in a dry summer, while others need water throughout their growing season or at key stages for worthwhile yields. To cut down on the work and waste, concentrate on watering those crops that will benefit most.

What needs watering?

Vegetables can be divided into three main groups according to how much water they need:

- Vegetables such as beetroot, cabbages, onions and parsnips, which show no real benefit from watering once established. Some may produce excessive leaves at the expense of edible roots if they are watered too often. Water only at the seedling or young plant stage.
- Vegetables that benefit from watering at a key stage in their growth, for example when they are producing fruits, pods or tubers. Watering before this will encourage only leafy growth.
- Vegetables such as lettuces, runner beans and spinach, which benefit from regular watering in dry weather to produce lush or succulent leaves or stems. Even these need a generous soaking only once a week rather than more frequent light sprinklings.

How much water?

After several weeks without rain, the soil surface will appear dry. However, before watering, dig a hole 13–15cm down. The chances are, particularly if you have used a mulch, that the soil lower down will feel damp and so will not need water. Soils that are dry 13–15cm down will need watering.

The amount of water needed for most vegetables in the second two groups above is 22 litres per sq m once a week. To convert this to a length of row, divide 1m by the inter-row spacing for that crop – giving you the length of row to receive that quantity of water. Lettuces with inter-row spacings of 30cm need 22 litres for every 3.3m length of row.

How to reduce watering

- Increase the water-holding ability of your soil either by adding organic matter as a mulch in spring or by making a trench the autumn before. In a drought, avoid digging the soil, as doing so will just dry it out further.

- Add a plastic sheet mulch for widely spaced crops such as brassicas or courgettes to conserve moisture.
- Hoe regularly to keep the surface of the soil dry and prevent evaporation from deeper in the soil.
- Draw up a ridge of soil around widely spaced crops. This helps water run into the ground rather than off the surface.
- Use funnels (made from plastic drinks bottles with their bottoms cut off) buried in the ground to direct water to the roots of crops.
- All vegetables in containers need to be watered. Move the plants to lightly shaded positions during periods of drought. Grouping them together and fitting them with automatic watering systems will help reduce the work.

Watering options

Use a watering can with a detachable rose, with the rose fitted so that the water comes out as a fine spray for young plants and seedlings. More mature crops can be watered without the rose. Direct a steady stream of water on to the soil, giving it time to soak in. The average watering can holds 10 litres.

Lay a leaky hose on the surface of the soil. Water seeps out of the sides. Leaky hoses are more efficient than sprinklers as the water is not scattered on foliage and in the air. They are flexible enough to be laid in various shapes, so are useful for small beds. It is easy to forget to turn them off, so consider using them with a water timer.

Automatic irrigation systems are useful when you are growing a lot of plants in containers (or in a greenhouse) and are not around to water them regularly. These can be used on the patio or in a greenhouse, and consist of a network of plastic tubing with small nozzles or drippers for each pot. They need to be set up and checked to ensure they are delivering the correct amount of water, and can be automated by using a watering computer fitted to the tap.

Water shortages

Water companies sometimes ban the use of sprinklers and hosepipes when water is in short supply, and some parts of the UK are particularly vulnerable. As a precaution, use an old water tank or barrel as a water reservoir near the vegetable plot. Keep it topped up before bans are imposed. During a water shortage, you can use cooled bath water and washing-up water as long as it is not too greasy. Water the ground and avoid getting it on the leaves.

USE SPACE EFFICIENTLY

In a small vegetable plot it is particularly important that you use every space to its best advantage. Try not to leave areas vacant and plan ahead so that when one crop is harvested another can be planted out to reoccupy the space. The five main techniques for using space efficiently are listed below.

Sow little and often

Rather than sow all the seed from a packet in one long row, sow a small proportion of it in a short row, small patch or couple of pots and repeat this every two or three weeks. This will help to provide a longer harvesting season and avoid a glut.

Double cropping

It should be possible to make efficient use of space by fitting two crops into the same area in one season. It also means that crops that suffer from pests and diseases later in the summer, such as peas with pea moth grubs and broad bean with chocolate spot, can be replaced in mid-summer by tender vegetables that are generally pest-free, such as dwarf beans and sweetcorn.

Any crop that is harvested in June, for example, shallots, early potatoes, the first sowings of calabrese and cauliflower, can be followed by tender vegetables started off in pots. Courgettes, cucumbers, marrows and squashes, tomatoes, sweetcorn and dwarf beans all fit the bill.

Later on in the summer, during July, overwintered vegetables can be planted to replace those harvested in early summer.

Early starters

Even the best-planned vegetable plots are likely to have bare soil in late winter and early spring. This is where cloches and the modern alternative, garden fleece, come in. By starting the hardiest crops in February or March, you can be certain that you will be able to follow them with another crop in early summer.

Catch crops

Small, fast-growing crops can be used as temporary space fillers. Particularly useful are beetroot, carrots, lettuces and spinach, which can be picked immature. The following examples show how catch crops can be used to increase the productivity of an area.

Between slow root crops Parsnips are notoriously slow to germinate and take months to fill their allotted space completely. Use quick crops of radishes, spring onions or short-rooted carrots between the rows of parsnips.

Between large brassicas Even if you start them in pots or a seedbed (see opposite) and transplant them, Brussels sprouts, sprouting broccoli, autumn cauliflower and kale all take a long time to fill their space. Use a related crop such as radish or lettuce to fill the space. If you start them earlier in the spring you should be able to get a crop of summer cabbage, cauliflower or calabrese. In this case, leave sufficient space to plant the winter brassicas between them.

Before tender crops Tomatoes, cucumbers and courgettes are planted out after the last likely frost and do not fill their allotted space for a couple of weeks. Use hardy catch crops from March or April until June.

Between rows of runner beans Runners beans are not sown or planted until late May or early June in most areas of the UK, although the supports may already be in place. So there is plenty of time to grow a quick crop of peas, lettuce or spinach before the beans start to cover their supports and cast too much shade.

Follow-on crops

By May, the vegetable plot is probably pretty full, but it is worth starting late or overwintered crops to follow those that will be harvested during June and July. All of them can be sown into small pots or a seedbed (see oppoise) and, provided they are kept well watered, will wait until you are ready to plant them out. Some of the best follow-on crops are broccoli, calabrese and cauliflower, which can all be sown in May and transplanted in July.

SOW OUTDOORS

Some vegetables are always sown directly into the ground or compost where they are to grow, notably carrots and parsnips, radishes and spring onions. Most other vegetables can either be sown direct or started off in pots, then planted out.

In many ways, sowing straight into the soil is easier as it saves having to look after large numbers of small plants in pots. However, direct-sown seedlings are more vulnerable to soil pests and diseases so it can be risky for expensive seed. Also, you have to wait for the soil to warm up, and this can delay sowing.

When to sow

Some vegetables are very hardy and can be sown outdoors early in the spring, while others are susceptible to frost and should not be sown outdoors until after the last frost normally occurs. Up to two weeks extra growing time can be gained by sowing outdoors early under cloches (see page 64).

Prepare a seedbed

1 Remove large stones, weeds or weed roots and break up large lumps of soil, either with the back of a garden fork or using a chopping action with a soil rake

2 Using a soil rake with a steady but gentle push-pull action, work the surface of the soil until it has a fine, even texture and is flat and level

3 Set out a garden line or pegs and string to mark the position of the rows. Use the correct row spacing for each vegetable (see under the individual entries). When planting different types of crops next to each other, allow for the different spacing. For example, if one crop needs 30cm and the next 60cm, leave 45cm between them, so the larger crop does not swamp the smaller one

preparation & techniques

Make a seed drill

A seed drill is a narrow trough into which you sow.

1 Using a string line and a narrow trowel (a pointing trowel is ideal), a cane or stick, or the corner of a draw hoe or soil rake, make a drill about 1.5cm deep

2 If the soil is very dry, dribble water into the bottom of the drill and allow it to soak in for a few minutes before sowing

Plant seeds

1 Open the seed packet and the inner foil packet carefully. Tip some seed into the palm of your hand. Take a pinch at a time and sow as evenly as you can into the bottom of the drill

2 Carefully draw soil over the seed drill to cover it. The soil should not need to be watered until the seedlings emerge

Some vegetables, such as radishes, spring onions and peas, are best sown in bands rather than single rows. Use a draw hoe with a blade 10–15cm wide to draw out a shallow trough. Sow the seed thinly so that they are evenly scattered across the width of the band.

Thinning seedlings

As soon as the seedlings are large enough to identify, pull out any that are surplus (this is called thinning out).

- Start by thinning larger clumps to one or two strong seedlings. Take care not to disturb the remaining seedlings too much.
- A couple of weeks later, remove all but one plant at about half or a third of the final spacing. For example, if the final spacing is 30cm, leave one plant every 10cm and pull two out later.
- With care, thinned seedlings can be replanted to fill any gaps.
- Thinnings of lettuces and carrots can be added to salads.

Transplanting

Some vegetables need so much space to mature that sowing them at their final spacings straight away would be a waste of valuable space. Cabbages, Brussels sprouts, winter cauliflower, kale and sprouting broccoli fall into this category. Leeks also transplant well.

Start such plants in a seedbed, but sown into short seed drills 15cm apart; thinning the seedlings to 5–10cm apart. When the plants reach 15cm high dig them up with as much root as possible and plant in their final position. These bare-root transplants may wilt at first but will quickly establish and grow to maturity. In dry weather, water the seedbed before lifting the transplants with a fork and water them well in their final position.

SOW INDOORS

Sowing indoors frees you from the vagaries of the weather and gives you much more control over seed germination. A greenhouse is the ideal place to start off vegetable seeds (see pages 59–60). It needs to be insulated and heated to prevent the temperature falling below freezing, or preferably keep it at about 3°–5°C. A coldframe is a cheaper alternative to a greenhouse for hardy vegetables that do not need high temperatures to germinate.

Tender vegetables are best started off on a warm windowsill where you can maintain a steady temperature of about 20°C. Ideally, it should get plenty of sunlight but preferably not full sun, which could easily scorch young seedlings. As the sunlight comes from one direction, the seedlings will bend towards it, so turn pots daily to keep the stems growing straight. Remember that if you draw the curtains at night, the windowsill temperature will drop considerably.

TIP
Remember to turn off a propagator without a thermostat on warm, sunny days.

Use a heated propagator for a cool room

A heated propagator consists of a plastic seed tray with a heating element built into it. This provides gentle bottom heat, which is usually capable of raising the temperature of the compost up to ten degrees

above the room temperature. This is useful for a cool room without central heating, a windowsill that gets cold at night when the curtains are drawn, or in a greenhouse. A transparent plastic top keeps the atmosphere moist; the best have adjustable ventilators to increase or decrease the humidity. Even the most powerful propagators will not be able to maintain 20°C if the room temperature drops much below 5°C, so background heating is essential in a greenhouse. It is worth checking the temperature in the greenhouse with a maximum-minimum thermometer.

Pots, trays or modules?

Plastic plant pots (7cm) are ideal for sowing most vegetable seed. Round pots are fine, but square ones can be fitted more neatly into trays if space is tight.

Modular trays are divided into square compartments and drop inside a standard seed tray. Those with 24 compartments are ideal for most vegetables, those with 40 will be more efficient for vegetables transplanted when quite small, such as lettuces.

TIP
Always label pots and trays with the variety name and date sown.

Sowing seeds

1 Fill the pot with multipurpose compost up to the level of the rim. Press the surface gently to firm it. Water gently, with a fine rose attached to the watering can, or stand the pot in a tray of water, to moisten the compost. Allow excess water to drain

2 Sow small seeds on to the compost surface or press larger ones into the compost. Scatter loose compost over the seeds, leaving roughly 0.5cm below the pot rim for watering

3 Cover the seeds with vermiculite (to the equivalent of thickness of the seed). This will keep the compost moist and help the seeds that need light for germination

4 Label, water carefully and pop into a plastic bag. Place on a sheltered windowsill or in a heated propagator

preparation & techniques

57

Pricking out

When a seed germinates, the first pair of leaves are actually part of the seed. The next pair to form are the first 'true' leaves and are more characteristic of the plant. Large seeds produce very large seed leaves and can be handled and pricked out as soon as they have fully opened. With smaller seeds, wait until at least one pair of true leaves has opened.

1 Prepare new pots full of firmed, moistened compost for the seedlings (see page 57)

2 Use a dibber or something thin and pointed (a plastic plant label works well) to ease individual seedlings gently out of the compost with as much root intact as possible

3 Hold them carefully by the tip of a leaf, never by the stem

TIP

When sowing small seeds, mix dust-like seeds with dry silver sand to aid sowing as it will show where you have sown.

4 Make a hole in the compost in a new pot and drop the root in. The seedling should end up at the same depth as it was in the original pot

5 Push the dibber into the compost beside the hole to firm the seedling in. Return the seedlings to a warm spot to recover

Potting on

Any vegetable that is likely to be in its pot for more than six weeks, or which grows very fast, is best transferred into a larger pot, say, 10cm. If the larger pot is also deeper, put a layer of compost in the bottom. Remove the plant with the ball of compost intact from the smaller pot. Do not pull the stem – put your hand over the top of the pot, with the plant stem between your index and middle fingers. Tap firmly on the bottom of the pot. Drop the plant plus compost into the larger pot and fill around it with fresh compost.

VEGETABLES IN THE GREENHOUSE

A greenhouse is not essential for growing vegetables, but if you want to grow a wide range of crops in reasonable quantities, it certainly makes life a lot easier.

Buying a greenhouse

Buy the largest greenhouse you can afford and can fit easily into the garden. Make sure it has several opening vents, preferably on both the roof and at floor level. Later in the summer, adequate ventilation is essential and a through draught is important.

You will need at least one bench for seed raising and shelves for growing on seedlings. Ideally, benches and shelves should be removable to allow crops to be grown in the greenhouse borders during the summer. Run an electricity supply to the greenhouse but remember that this is a job for a professional.

Keep it frost-free

To grow vegetables throughout the winter, you will need to keep the greenhouse frost-free. The best way to do this is by using a thermostatically controlled electric fan heater set to about 3°C to provide background heating. If you use the greenhouse mainly from spring onwards for seed raising, you can screen off part of it with a curtain of bubble polythene and heat only that area.

Growing crops

The best place to grow greenhouse vegetables is in a soil border rather than on a bench. This gives them more headroom, which is particularly important for cordon tomatoes, and makes watering easier.

Enrich the border soil with a mulch of garden compost or well-rotted manure each spring. Also alternate unrelated crops, such as tomatoes and cucumbers, between borders each year. This will help prevent the build-up of soil diseases. If you notice a fall in yield and the plants look unhealthy, you may need to switch to growing them in large pots or growing bags.

Both large pots and growing bags contain enough nutrients to support a vigorous plant (such as a tomato

TRY THIS

Fix bubble polythene insulation material to the greenhouse frame to help reduce heat loss. Drape a piece over the door and, if possible, run it across the roof space at head height to reduce the area to be heated. Start to remove the insulation material from the south side of the greenhouse in late spring to allow maximum light in.

preparation & techniques

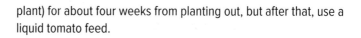

plant) for about four weeks from planting out, but after that, use a liquid tomato feed.

Watering

Check your plants each day to see if they need watering. Stick your finger into the compost and rub it at the base of your thumb where the skin is sensitive. If it feels damp, don't water and if it feels dry, give it a good soak. It's best to water in the morning as excess water in the evening tends to hang around and can lead to rots and mould.

Alternatively, invest in a watering system, which comprises a reservoir and tubing that trickles water into the pots or growing bags. More sophisticated systems are attached to a garden tap and feed water to plants via a thin tubing and adjustable nozzles. Such systems can be automated with the addition of a timer or water computer. This means that even if you go away, the greenhouse will be watered each day.

Hygiene

Clear out the greenhouse once a year, in late autumn or winter, and clean it thoroughly. Scrub the frame and glass (including the gaps between the glass sheets) with a greenhouse disinfectant or hot soapy water to remove algae and grime. Cleaning ensures plenty of light reaches the crops but also removes overwintering pests inside. Clean and disinfect all pots and trays used for raising seedlings, as well as the propagator and benches.

If you start the seeds in clean conditions you reduce the risk of damping-off disease. This fungus strikes vulnerable seedlings, which then fall over, often in patches. If you can catch the disease early enough, watering with a solution of a copper-based fungicide should prevent it spreading to healthy seedlings.

5 MINUTE JOB

Damp down the greenhouse floor Bright sunny days can send the temperature soaring so damp down the floor with water and open vents and windows.

Other problems that affect greenhouse crops, such as aphids and spider mites, can be effectively dealt with by biological controls rather than by using chemical controls (see page 43).

BUY PLANTS

When you want only a couple of tomato plants or a few lettuces for a container, it makes sense to buy them as young plants rather than raise your own from seed. Alternatively, you may want to save the hassle of sowing seed and you can buy collections of veg plants online to fill a whole plot. When deciding which to buy, look at what the collections include, such as the number of plants of each vegetable. Most need to be ordered by March and are sent out during May and early June.

Most of the common vegetables are widely available in plant form, and the choice of varieties is generally good, especially for tomatoes. You may find only run-of-the-mill varieties in some garden centres. If you want new or unusual varieties, order young plants from a mail-order catalogue or website.

When to buy

In most garden centres, young vegetable plants are bought in and displayed throughout the spring. Like bedding plants, many tender vegetable plants are put on sale in March even though they cannot be planted out until the end of May. This makes caring for the young plants a lot more work than it needs to be as you have to keep them frost-free and will probably have to pot them on into larger pots at least once to prevent a check to their growth. However, if you wait until May before buying, you may be disappointed by the quality of the plants left in the shops. There is also the danger that shops will have sold out.

What to look for

Plants that you might want only one or two of (aubergines, courgettes, cucumbers, marrows, sweet peppers and tomatoes, for example) are sold singly in small pots. However, crops such as lettuces, cabbages and sweetcorn, where several plants are needed for a decent yield, tend to be sold in strips of about a dozen plants.

It is worth shopping around, not just to compare prices, but because some outlets have purpose-built facilities to keep plants well-lit yet frost-free, while others display them in outdoor areas, where they may get frosted, or indoors where light levels are inadequate. By following the advice overleaf, you can make sure you obtain top-quality plants.

🌱 Always buy freshly delivered stock, as plants soon dry out and deteriorate when they are kept in small volumes of compost for several weeks.

🌱 Look for stocky or bushy plants with healthy green foliage. Straggly or leggy plants have been deprived of light and should be avoided. Also avoid plants with unnatural, discoloured foliage; this is a sign of stress, frost or lack of nutrients.

🌱 Avoid cauliflower and calabrese, which can easily suffer a check to growth and bolt.

🌱 Avoid bringing pests into the garden: greenfly or blackfly can gather in the young growth. Speckled cucumber and courgette foliage is a sign of spider mite. Yellow or crinkled leaves could also indicate virus disease – avoid these, too.

🌱 Avoid buying bare-rooted brassica plants to reduce the likelihood of introducing clubroot into your soil.

Aftercare

Hardy plants, such as lettuces and brassicas, can be planted outside straight away unless they were displayed indoors, in which case they need to be hardened off (for about a week) before planting (see opposite).

Tender vegetables (courgettes, marrows, runner beans, sweetcorn) need to be kept in a light, frost-free place then hardened off for ten days before planting after the

last frost date. If planting out is delayed more than a couple of weeks, pot on into larger pots or apply a dilute liquid feed.

Greenhouse vegetables, such as tomatoes, cucumbers and peppers, should be kept in a light, frost-free place, ideally in a heated greenhouse. They do not need potting on, but aim to plant them into their final pots or growing bags by May. Feed with a tomato feed if you keep them in the same pots for more than four weeks.

Hardening off

A coldframe is the ideal place to get plants used to outdoor conditions gradually, over a period of seven to ten days. First leave the plants in the coldframe with the top closed for a day, then open the top slightly the second day but close it at night. Repeat this, opening the top wider each day until it is wide open during the day. Then start opening the top slightly at night, increasing this until the plants are acclimatised to outdoor conditions (the foliage will look healthy and the plants will be growing).

TRY THIS

It is often harder to sow seed in summer than in spring as you need to remember to sow late crops and it can be difficult to keep the soil or pots of compost moist in hot weather. Fortunately, several seed companies will now despatch young plants of autumn or winter greens in summer. This is a useful way to catch up and ensure you have fresh produce during the autumn and winter months.

preparation & techniques

Use a double layer of garden fleece and a sheltered paved area near a greenhouse or on a patio instead of a coldframe. Leave first one layer then both layers of fleece off for increasing amounts of time during the day, then at night.

FROST PROTECTION

Warming the air and soil around plants means you can start growing crops earlier in the year and continue for longer at the end of the season. This is especially useful if you live in a cold area or have to cope with a cold, wet soil. Cloches also protect plants and soil from heavy rain and wind.

The two main structures used to protect plants are cloches and coldframes, both of which are made of glass or various types of plastic. Cloches can be moved about to protect seeds and plants growing in the ground, while a coldframe provides conditions that are halfway between those in the greenhouse and those outside. It is used to protect plants prior to planting out. Garden fleece is now widely used to protect plants from frost.

Cloches

You can buy a ready-to-use cloche or buy cloche clips and then get your own glass cut to fit. If you have raised beds, it is worth making your own cloche to sit on the beds. Do this by creating a series of hoops (made from overflow piping) and position them 60cm apart along the length of the vegetable bed. Then cover the hoops with polythene sheeting. When choosing a ready-to-use cloche, consider the following:

- Match the cloche to your site. Bell jars and lantern cloches make attractive features in borders, potagers or other ornamental areas. Other cloches are best in vegetable plots and allotments – most are designed to cover rows of vegetables. Some designs are prone to being blown away, so in windy sites look for a design that can be firmly secured to the ground.
- Match the cloche to your crop. Small tent cloches 30–45cm wide are useful for getting seedlings and young plants off to a good start, but plants soon outgrow them. Tunnel cloches or barn cloches are a better shape for more mature plants.
- A cloche should be convenient to use. It should be easy to tend the crop and to move the cloche. You will need to ventilate the cloche on warm, sunny days, either by removing the whole cover, taking off the sides or adjusting the panels or flaps.

Coldframes

A coldframe is like a large box and provides an environment halfway between indoors and outdoors (see page 63). It is usually placed near a greenhouse. It saves you time as you do not need to keep moving trays of young plants outdoors during the day and back indoors in the evening, and so is worth considering if you grow a reasonable amount of tender plants (this could include bedding plants as well as vegetables).

Garden fleece

Garden fleece is sold in packs or rolls and can be used in place of cloches or coldframes. Lay it over plants after sowing or planting or while getting them used to outdoor conditions. A double layer of fleece will protect plants from frost when the outside temperature is down to -4°C. Fleece is more versatile than a fixed structure but it needs to be secured well at the edges and is prone to ripping. Remove the fleece once the weather gets warm. Top-quality fleece can be washed in the washing machine and re-used several times.

Extending the season

In the spring, if you use cloches, you can sow or plant a whole range of crops such as lettuces, carrots, spring onions and radishes earlier than normal, although you still need to check the soil temperature. Put the cloches in position two weeks in advance of sowing or planting, so the soil has a chance to dry out slightly and warm up.

In summer, make an August sowing of summer lettuces in a cloche or coldframe. Start them off with the cloche ends removed or the coldframe top removed. Cover the crop when the first frost is forecast.

In autumn, cloches can be placed over growing crops to encourage ripening or to preserve leaf quality. For example, large cloches are put over tomatoes or courgettes in late September to extend cropping into the autumn. Cordon tomatoes need to be untied from their supports and laid on sheet mulch before they are covered.

THE PEA FAMILY

Peas and beans of all kinds are vegetable plot essentials. Between them, they'll give you a supply all through the summer months and any surplus can be frozen easily. They belong to a plant group called legumes. A common feature is their ability to 'fix' nitrogen from the air onto their roots to feed themselves. For a gardener, this is useful because it means they don't need much fertiliser.

GOOD VARIETIES

'Ambassador' (shelling peas)

'Carouby de Maussanne' (very tall variety of mangetout)

'Delikett' (sugar snap peas)

'Oregon Sugar Pod' (fairly tall variety for mangetout)

PEAS

Fresh garden peas are a treat compared to the ubiquitous frozen type. Do not be put off by the thought of having to shell them – you can eat mangetout and snap peas, pod and all. Peas can be grown in several ways: train taller varieties up a wigwam, trellis or against a fence. Grow dwarf ones in a container or even a hanging basket. Mangetout are good value – you should get around 2kg per sq m of this tasty vegetable, which is reasonably expensive to buy.

Preparing and caring

Crop rotation Peas and beans are an important part of a crop rotation system and occupy one of the four rotation groups, usually between two of the greedier groups: potatoes and brassicas (see pages 21–3).

Peas thrive on deep, well-drained soil with plenty of organic matter On poor soil, it is worth preparing a trench over winter and filling it with a mixture of soil and well-rotted organic matter. Since peas manufacture their own nitrogen fertiliser from the air through the nodules on their roots, they need no additional feeding.

Early planting In a cold spring, try starting the seeds in a greenhouse or other sheltered spot in February or March. But instead of using pots,

look for flat-bottomed plastic guttering. Cut it into lengths that fit into your veg plot or raised beds, but that are no longer than 1.5m. Block each end with a brick and three-quarters fill with compost. Sow the seeds in three rows about 5cm apart each way and cover with compost. Keep the compost just moist. After a couple of weeks when the tops are 5cm or so tall, dig a shallow trough into the ground with a hoe and slide the contents of the guttering into it.

Alternatively, sow the seed into bands rather than single rows Make a 2cm-deep trough about 10cm wide and scatter the seeds roughly 5cm apart. Cover and keep the soil moist. All but the very dwarf varieties benefit from support. Put this in place

before the seedlings appear. The traditional approach is to use twiggy branches or 'pea sticks'. An alternative is plastic pea netting strung between posts.

Cropping times Taller varieties are likely to crop over a longer period than the shorter varieties from a single sowing. However, by making several sowings of the shorter varieties throughout the summer, you can prolong cropping. An alternative is to make one sowing of an early and a maincrop variety.

5 MINUTE JOB

Give your peas support All but the very dwarf varieties will need support of some kind. Tall varieties will need very solid supports. Twiggy branches called pea sticks are the traditional solution – simply push them into the rows. If you cannot get these, use lengths of pea and bean netting securely tied to posts. It is always easier to put the supports in place before or shortly after the seedlings emerge.

Mice love newly sown peas and broad beans and work along the rows – use traps or bait if they become a nuisance.

Pea moth usually goes unnoticed until you start shelling the peas. One or more of the peas has been burrowed into by a small white grub, which is usually still inside the pod. To prevent this happening, cover the crop with fine mesh; concentrate on early sowings.

Pea and bean weevil nibble the edges of the leaves, but rarely cause enough damage to affect the yield.

Harvesting and storing

Mangetout

Pick mangetout varieties regularly as soon as they reach 5cm and before they start to become stringy.

Shelling peas

Pick these when the pods are plump and the peas inside are full-sized but still tender. Pick a few test pods to help judge the optimum stage.

SOWING AND GROWING

February	In mild areas, it is worth making an early sowing under cloches or garden fleece. Take precautions against mice (see opposite). In colder areas, start peas off in small pots, modular trays or lengths of guttering in the greenhouse (see page 68) or coldframe (see page 65).
March	Sow tall peas for the ornamental border in pots under cover. Sow a couple of seeds per 7cm pot and do not worry if more than one comes up. Make the first outdoor sowings in milder areas. Peas are normally sown in wide (10cm) drills about 2.5–5cm deep. Sow seed thinly, aiming for one every 5cm each way. If you prefer, sow single rows with seeds 5cm apart or triple rows with seeds 12cm apart. Allow 60cm between adjacent rows or bands, slightly more for taller varieties.
April	Plant tall varieties in the border, about 12cm apart, alongside their supports. Make outdoor sowings in colder areas, covering with garden fleece if severe weather is forecast. Peas will germinate at 4°C, but nearer 10°C is preferable. Try growing a crop in a container. Aim for eight plants to a 10-litre pot, sowing a few more seed to allow for failures. Push a couple of twiggy sticks into the pot for support.
May	The earliest crop should be ready. Pick frequently, removing all the pods that are ready. Leaving pods on the plants for too long will shorten the cropping season.
June	Peas that are in flower now are at risk from pea moth (see opposite) but peas sown now should escape damage. If the soil is very dry, a good soaking when the plants are in full flower and the first pods are starting to form will increase the yield.
July	Later crops are still at risk from pea moth. It may be worth a very late sowing in milder areas: use an early quick-maturing variety.
August–September	Keep picking over later sowings regularly. When the crop is finished, cut the tops off the plants at ground level and add to the compost heap.
October–November	Sow the hardiest varieties for a very early crop the following spring. These plants are guaranteed to be free of pea moth. Use spare borders in the greenhouse for an overwintering crop of mangetout peas.

RUNNER BEANS

Runner beans are one of the most popular garden vegetables. A dozen plants will supply enough beans for a family over the summer, even if you don't grow any other crops. They are both decorative and versatile and can fit into any garden: in the ornamental border, as a temporary summer screen or as a container crop.

The ideal site for runner beans is sunny and sheltered from strong winds. They are even worth trying in partial shade. The soil should be kept moist. Grow them up teepees made of bamboo canes, trellis screens, over arches or against a sunny fence. When growing them on a vegetable plot, choose a position where they will not be casting shade over other vegetables. In an ornamental border, leave room for access, since you may need to pick every other day.

Preparing and caring

Good soil preparation is the key Dig a trench to improve poor soil (see page 34). Then, two weeks before planting out scatter a little general-purpose fertiliser across the vegetable plot and then water the ground a day or two before sowing if the soil is dry.

Sow or plant two seeds or plants to each support at 15cm intervals.

You may need to protect the young plants from slugs (see pages 40–1).

Sow the large seeds individually in pots. Don't sow too many runner beans – a wigwam of just 12 plants can yield 6kg!

Twine the lead shoots of French and runner beans to the canes as they start to grow, winding them anti-clockwise. Make sure you follow their natural direction and tie them in if necessary.

5MINUTE JOB

Water regularly in dry weather
Give a generous soaking – 10 litres of water per sq m once a week. Watering encourages flowering and increases the size of the pods. However, spraying the flowers to aid setting is a waste of time.

Dwarf runner beans You can grow any runner bean variety as a bush, like dwarf French beans (see page 76). Sow them 15cm apart in rows 60cm apart. Pinch off the growing tip when each plant reaches 30cm. Keep removing any climbing shoots regularly and soon you will have dwarf bushes that should start cropping a fortnight earlier than normal.

A few true dwarf varieties are also available. They do not produce climbing shoots. These are worth growing if you have a very exposed garden, want to grow beans in containers or want to grow them under cloches for an early crop. However, the yield is disappointing compared to climbing beans, and the pods trail on the soil.

Blackfly can build up rapidly later in the summer and in severe cases can stunt the plants and reduce the crop (see page 83).

Halo blight is the only disease you are likely to come across. This shows as dark spots on the leaves, surrounded by a paler halo. Pull out and destroy any affected plants as soon as you spot them. Do not save seed for next year as this disease is carried in the seeds.

No pods Flowers sometimes fail to produce pods. Cool spells may discourage pollinating insects, or high nightime temperatures or drought could cause the embryo beans to abort. Water the soil on hot, dry evenings. Do not bother spraying the flowers – it will not help. Varieties that set pods without pollination by insects are now available.

TIP

To grow beans up a fence, trellis, arch or pergola you can use bean netting.

Provide good support There are many options when it comes to supporting runner beans. Choose a method that suits where you plan to grow them.

- In a small garden or in a mixed border, a simple wigwam of beanpoles (coppiced hazel is ideal if you can get it) or bamboo canes is best. Make the base at least 60cm diameter or square and space supports 15cm apart. Tie them securely at the top – or use a plastic wigwam grip. You can substitute intermediate sticks with twine or string. Wigwams should be at least 1.8m tall, so you will need 2m canes.
- In sheltered gardens, a single row of canes or poles should be adequate. You could also erect a couple of stout posts and stretch string supports or pea and bean netting from them.
- In exposed gardens, double rows are more secure. Space the bases of the rows 60cm apart and brace the supports together, crossing near the top. A variation on this theme is to angle the canes, supporting them halfway up with a cross member, so that the beans hang down clear of the supports. Strengthen the structure further by tying canes or poles horizontally where the uprights cross.
- Whatever method you choose, space plants 15cm apart or pairs of plants 30cm apart.

Harvesting and storing

Pick the beans regularly when they reach about 17–18cm long. If you let them grow too large they will become tough and stringy, and cropping will fall off. Pick every bean, even if you cannot eat or freeze them all, to prolong cropping into late summer. Before you go on holiday, pick all the beans, even the tiniest ones, and the flowers, to ensure a continuing crop when you return.

SOWING AND GROWING

March	Put the supports in place now (see opposite), to save time later. To utilise the space between bean double rows, or in the middle of wigwams, sow a catch crop of lettuce, spinach or even early peas. These should be out of the way by the time the beans need the space.
April	In milder areas, sow the beans in pots. Sow two seeds to a 12cm pot. Keep the pots at a constant 10–12°C. If both germinate, do not separate them later, but plant both together. Grow them on at a minimum temperature of 7°C until they are 15–20cm tall.
May	Gradually harden off the young plants (see page 63), ready for planting out later in the month in milder areas. You could also sow the seed directly into the soil or in containers after the danger of late frost has passed. Sow 2cm deep when the soil is 10°C. Sow or plant two or three plants to a 10-litre pot. Push a tripod of 1.8m canes into the pot or stand next to a trellis. In colder areas: sow seeds in pots this month for planting out in early June.
June	Sow directly or plant out in colder areas. In exposed areas: protect young plants from cold winds until they are well established. Mulch around the plants with well-rotted manure, compost or grass cuttings to help retain moisture and suppress weeds. Water well in dry spells.
July	When the plants reach the top of their supports, pinch out their tips, to encourage side shoots to grow. Watch for blackfly (see opposite). Make a second sowing, if you have room, to prolong cropping into October.
August–September	Harvest beans regularly (see above).

GOOD VARIETIES

'Amethyst' (thin purple pods)

'Green Arrow' (good yield and quality)

'Speedy' (quick, fine pods)

'Stanley' (good yield and quality)

DWARF FRENCH BEANS

If you enjoy those expensive beans imported from Kenya or exotic sounding dried beans such as borlotti, why not try growing your own? Both types are easy to grow, take up little room, and some are ornamental, too. You can produce a succession of beans throughout the summer, and harvest your own haricot beans (dried beans) in the autumn.

Dwarf French beans are a trouble-free crop with several advantages over runner beans. They do not need insects to pollinate the flowers, which makes them ideal as early or late crops under glass. The plants are compact so only limited support is needed and they are small enough to grow early under cloches if you do not have a greenhouse.

Preparing and caring

French beans are very sensitive to frost. It is not worth sowing outdoors until the risk of frost has passed. French beans need a minimum soil temperature of 10°C in order to germinate. Check the temperature about 1.5cm deep with a soil thermometer before you risk sowing. Do this in the early morning and wait until a mild, settled spell is forecast before sowing.

Start off in pots Sow 3–4 seeds per small pot or modular seed tray. Don't bother to thin them out, but just plant them as a clump.

Use cloches You can sow directly into the soil under cloches, in which case put them in place at least two weeks before to warm the soil.

When the first flowers start to form, regular watering will greatly increase the yield in dry periods. Give a thorough soaking once a week or fortnight to wet the soil to a good depth when they start to flower.

5 MINUTE JOB

If seeds start to mature in unpicked pods, flowering will cease. Pick and discard any surplus pods to prolong the harvest.

In colder areas towards the end of the season, cover the latest sowings with cloches or garden fleece to protect them against unexpected frosts.

Blackfly starts to build up rapidly as the weather warms up, from June onwards (see page 83).

Mice are often responsible for gaps in rows of direct-sown beans. Set traps or sow extra seeds to allow gaps to be filled later.

Mosaic virus is common across many plants. It is spread by aphids and results in puckered leaves with yellow veins. In severe cases plants become stunted and the fruits inedible. Lift and destroy the plants to prevent it spreading. There is no cure.

Slugs will also attack the young plants and later the young pods (see pages 40–1).

Harvesting and storing

Pick pods as soon as they reach 10cm for pencil-pod varieties, or at no more than 15cm for larger, flat-podded types. Take care that you do not pull too hard or you will loosen the plant in its hole in the ground.

To enjoy dwarf beans at their best, eat them straight away and take care not to overcook them. Surplus beans can be blanched and frozen for winter use.

For dried beans, leave them until mid-autumn. Cover the plants with cloches in wet spells and pick them and bring indoors if frost threatens. You can continue drying in a sunny, airy room or in a greenhouse if necessary. Eventually, the pods will be dry and brittle and then seeds can be easily separated and stored in jars.

You may come across soya beans in specialist seed catalogues. Grow them just as you would dwarf French beans. The plants look very similar, but their seeds give them away.

They produce small, green or black flat pods with usually only two small round seeds. Do not expect huge yields in the UK.

SOWING AND GROWING

March	If you have empty greenhouse borders and are prepared to provide background heating to keep the temperature above 5°C at night, you should be able to get a quick crop of dwarf beans before planting out your tomatoes in May. Follow the general sowing advice given below and grow four plants in a 10-litre container.
April	You can sow the seed in pots under cover about four weeks before it is safe to plant outdoors. In milder areas, sow the seed in 7cm pots or modular trays for an early crop outdoors. Under cloches: sow in blocks with 15cm between seeds each way.
May	In colder areas, make the main sowing in pots now for planting out into containers and ornamental borders as well as the vegetable plot. In milder areas, plant out beans started in pots in April. You could also sow directly into the soil. Sow or plant in rows 30cm apart, with plants 7.5cm apart. Sow two or three seeds each time to allow for any failures. Pull out any surplus seedlings later. In borders: allow a diameter of 15cm for each plant. In containers: allow about four plants to a 30cm diameter pot.
June	Plant out seeds started in pots in May in colder areas. Sow a late crop directly into the soil in all areas. These will crop into September.
July–August	As soon as pods start to form, keep picking them regularly, twice a week if necessary. Dwarf beans may need some support to stop them flopping over. If necessary, push twigs into the soil along the rows or use twine tied to canes pushed in at intervals. Make a final outdoor sowing in milder areas if there is space in the vegetable plot. Give the seedbed a really thorough watering first.
October	For dried beans, leave the plants as long as possible before harvesting.

GOOD VARIETIES

'Blue Lake' (flat pods)

'Cobra' (slim pods)

'Neckar Gold' (yellow pods)

'Violet Podded' (purple pods)

CLIMBING FRENCH BEANS

As a change from runner beans, try growing climbing French beans up a wigwam in the border or on a trellis or arch. Varieties with yellow-, purple- and red-flushed pods are available, as well as the plain green ones. Most have white flowers, though some have pale mauve blooms.

Climbing French beans and runner beans both originated in South America and were brought back to Europe in the 16th century. The British favoured the runner bean (*Phaseolus coccineus*), while elsewhere in Europe, *Phaseolus vulgaris* was preferred, which led to the common name of French bean. French beans tend to give a better crop early in the season, but are then overtaken by runners later on.

Preparing and caring
Enrich the soil by digging in well-rotted manure or garden compost, as for runners.

Prepare supports, unless you are using an existing garden structure. Simplest is a wigwam of bamboo canes or bean poles. Erect it so there is a base of at least 60cm diameter, with the supports spaced 15cm apart and tied securely at the top. French beans are not as vigorous as runners – supports 1.8m high should be sufficient. You can substitute strings for alternate canes if you prefer. They can also be grown in long rows like runner beans (see pages 72–4).

Harvesting and storing

Snap a bean to check it breaks cleanly. Harvest while tender and before the beans inside have started to swell – if you let the beans mature, flowering and continued cropping will drop off.

After picking, tie in stray shoots to keep plants neat.

HEALTH WATCH!

See page 78 for the pests that most affect dwarf French beans; the same pests and diseases apply here.

SOWING AND GROWING

April–May	Sow the seed, two in a 7cm pot, under cover (see page 77 for more details).
June	Plant out after the danger of frost has passed. You can also sow seed directly into the soil this month. Sow two or three seeds, or one plant, 15cm apart. Ideally, each plant should have its own support.
July–August	As with runner beans, pick the pods regularly when they are still tender.
September–October	Towards the end of the season, leave some of the pods to mature. These will become dry and brittle and the beans inside can then be harvested for use as haricot beans or saved for next year's crop. French beans do not usually have the nitrogen-fixing nodules of runner beans.

 # The Pea Family

GOOD VARIETIES

'Aquadulce Claudia' (for autumn sowing)

'Scorpio' (small-seeded)

'Witkiem Manita' (earliest spring sown)

BROAD BEANS

It can be difficult to buy good-quality fresh broad beans in the shops. But this needn't worry the vegetable gardener, as broad beans are easy to grow and, unlike runner beans, they are hardy, so there is the option of sowing in either autumn or spring. The dwarf varieties are free-standing so they can be grown in gaps in beds and borders where the blue-green foliage and white or purple flowers are an attractive feature early in the season.

Preparing and caring

Broad beans grow early in the year, so they need an open, sunny site with shelter from strong winds. As their roots fix nitrogen from the air, they are a useful part of a crop rotation and can be followed by a greedy feeder such as one of the cabbage family (see pages 21–3).

Sowing in pots In cold areas or poor soil, get a head start by sowing seeds individually in pots and planting out later.

On a vegetable plot, broad beans are usually grown in double rows with plants 20cm apart each way. A path of 60cm between double rows makes for easier picking. If you prefer, you can grow single rows 45cm apart, with plants 13cm apart. Broad beans can also be grown in a block, with plants 20–30cm apart each way.

When growing a row, it is quicker to use a draw hoe to take out a seed drill 5cm deep. Sow more than you need at the end of each row. You can then transplant these to fill in any gaps.

Dwarf varieties do not need support but tall varieties may lean over, so a length of string along the rows secured by canes or stakes makes access easier.

Broad beans do not need watering before the flowers appear, but it is worth hoeing to keep the weeds down when the plants are small. If it is very dry when the flowers are forming, a good soak once a week (22 litres a sq m) will improve the quality of the final crop.

When planting seeds in November, choose a sheltered spot with well-drained soil if possible. Much depends on where you are and the kind of winter you get as to their success, so keep some seeds back for sowing in spring.

broad beans

HEALTH WATCH!

Bean seed beetle grubs can make holes in the seed if you save seed for next year. Unless severely damaged they should still germinate.

Bean seed fly maggots live in the soil and can damage the young seedlings. If this is a problem, start the seeds off in pots.

Blackfly breed rapidly around the growing tips from May onwards. You might also find leaves that are sticky and covered with a black sooty mould. Spray severe infestations. If you spot the colonies early enough, pinch out the growing tips, together with blackfly, regularly.

Cont. on page 84

The Pea Family

Cont. from page 83

HEALTH WATCH!

Broad bean rust looks similar to chocolate spot (see below), but the spots are powdery and more likely in the summer. Treat as for chocolate spot.

Chocolate spot results in chocolate-coloured spots on the leaves and stems. It is most likely to occur on overwintered plants during a wet spring. Pick off and destroy badly affected leaves.

Mice relish broad bean seeds. To deter them dip the seed in paraffin and put layers of prickly leaves, such as holly, over the seed drills. Plants started off in pots indoors are less likely to be damaged.

Pea and bean weevil cut semi-circular notches out of the edges of the leaves. Plants may look ragged, but usually outgrow the damage. Use an insecticide if the damage is severe.

Harvesting and storing

Pick the lower pods first as they mature. For shelling, pick the pods when the seeds inside are just showing and are still soft. You can also pick the young, tender pods and eat them whole, like French beans. To test the pods are at the right stage for shelling, open one up and look at the scar where the seed is joined to the pod – it should be green or white. The beans are past their best if the scar is discoloured. Pull the pods downwards (try twisting them at the same time), but if they prove difficult to break off revert to cutting them off, otherwise you may damage the main stem or even uproot the plant.

Spread the harvest by picking early and regularly to avoid a glut. The worst that can happen is that you end up freezing the surplus to enjoy later in the year.

Blanch surplus broad beans in boiling water and freeze them. Any pods that are left to dry on the plant can be opened and the dry beans stored and used in stews. You can also save seed for planting next year (from healthy plants only). Note that they may cross-pollinate with other broad beans growing nearby.

Keep picking them regularly until no more pods are produced. Cut the top growth for the compost heap, but leave the roots in the ground.

SOWING AND GROWING

March	Make the first outdoor sowing in March, as soon as the soil is workable. You could start earlier in February by sowing under cloches or garden fleece. In cold areas or to give the plants a good head start: sow seed, one per 7cm pot, in a greenhouse or coldframe. Use a trowel, or push the seeds in 2cm deep with your finger. In a border: plant informal drifts of three to five plants 15–20cm apart. In a container: grow plants by simply pushing four seeds into a 10-litre pot in spring.
April	April is the last chance to sow spring-sown beans. In theory, it is possible to sow broad beans later for a summer or autumn crop, but these late crops are likely to suffer from severe attacks of chocolate spot and yields can be very poor. Plant out beans that were started in pots, after careful hardening off (see page 63).
May	When the plants are in full flower, pinch out the top 10cm. This encourages the pods to form and reduces problems with blackfly (see page 83). The first crops can be ready in June if you sowed in February or the previous autumn (see October).
June	This is the main harvesting time (see opposite). In a border: remove the plants after harvesting and replace them with late-flowering perennials such as penstemons.
July–August	On a vegetable plot: dig spent plants into the soil to provide green manure.
October	If you have a sheltered garden or live in a mild area, hardy varieties such as 'Aquadulce Claudia' can be sown now (or up to December) for an early crop next year, but keep half of the seed for a conventional spring sowing in case the winter is cold and damp. Sow in double rows or blocks with 20cm between plants each way. Or start broad beans in pots under cover for planting outside in early spring.

SALAD CROPS

These days, salad means more than just lettuce. One of the pleasures of growing your own is that you can easily grow a wide range of tasty leaf crops to rival the bagged supermarket salads. They are also among the quickest of crops and are a great way to fill in between slow-growing vegetables or unoccupied spaces. Add some cucumbers and asparagus and you're away.

Salad Crops

LETTUCE

Lettuce is the perfect crop for a window box or other container, and needs little care, other than regular watering. You can grow any variety of lettuce in an ornamental border or bed, though the loose-leaved and coloured kinds are the best choice as a foliage edging. In a small raised vegetable bed, growing lettuce is a very efficient use of space, and by regular sowing you can easily achieve a constant supply of tasty, fresh salad leaves for your salads (see also page 90).

Preparing and caring

Lettuces grow best in a sunny but sheltered spot early in the year. In the summer, they will tolerate light shade, and may bolt prematurely in full sun. In a vegetable plot, try to grow them in a different part of the plot each year or incorporate them into a crop rotation (see pages 21–3) in case soil pests or diseases start to build up.

A neutral soil with plenty of organic matter is best, so grow them with the cabbage family (see pages 148–79). During the summer they can be used to fill in between slow-growing winter crops, for example, Brussels sprouts, sprouting broccoli, winter cauliflower.

In pots or containers, lettuce thrive in a multipurpose compost, provided it is kept moist. Allowing the compost to dry out will encourage the plants to bolt. A 15–20cm pot is large enough to grow a lettuce to maturity, provided it is kept well watered and fed weekly with a high-nitrogen fertiliser. In larger containers allow about 23cm between plants, or grow closer together for a crop of loose leaves.

lettuce

5 MINUTE JOB

When planting lettuces in a border, treat them just like bedding plants but work a small amount of a balanced fertiliser into the soil before planting and water thoroughly if the soil is dry.

HEALTH WATCH!

Cutworms sever the stems of young plants at ground level and are rarely visible. Lettuces in containers are unlikely to be attacked.

Downy mildew occurs particularly in cool, wet summers and on greenhouse lettuce. Leaves become mottled yellow with a white downy mould on the undersides. Remove affected leaves and thin out to increase air circulation. Avoid wetting the leaves.

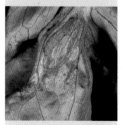

Cont. on page 90

HEALTH WATCH!

Cont. from page 89

Lettuce aphids attack plants in containers as well as in the garden. Check the undersides of the leaves occasionally and if numbers start to build up and natural predators such as ladybirds and hoverfly larvae cannot keep up, you may have to spray (see page 41).

Slugs and snails nibble irregular holes in the leaves at night (see pages 40–1).

Tip burn is caused by poor movement of calcium within the plant and shows as watery edges to the inner leaves, which turn brown and rot. Keep the plants well watered in hot, dry weather to prevent this problem.

Plant out the earliest sowing under cloches or fleece, which should be put in place a week or two before to help warm up the soil. Water the soil if it is dry. Remove cloches from the earliest sowing in April. These should be ready from May to June, depending on the type. In colder areas, also cover autumn crops with cloches. In all areas, cover winter lettuces with cloches.

If you plant at fortnightly intervals, from June onwards you should be rewarded with a steady supply of lettuces throughout the summer. As the summer progresses, later sowings will catch up with earlier ones. However, seeds, especially butterhead types, may fail to germinate in high summer when the temperature is over 20°C. To overcome this, sow in the late afternoon, so that the critical stage of germination occurs in the cool of evening.

Lettuces will not necessarily produce small hearts if grown closer together, unlike some other vegetables. You are more likely to end up with a mass of leaves.

If you want small lettuce hearts, choose a naturally small variety, such as 'Little Gem' and space them just 15–23cm apart. These are a good choice for growing in pots, window boxes or mini-vegetable beds. Each plant should make a heart about 7.5cm across, which is ideal for a salad for two.

Harvesting and storing

Harvest lettuces in the early morning, when the leaves are turgid, and store in a plastic bag in the fridge to keep them cool and moist. To check that hearted lettuce is ready, lay the back of your hand on top and press gently – it should feel firm.

SOWING AND GROWING

February	Make the earliest sowing under cover. Sow two or three seeds together, about 1.5cm deep, in small pots or modular seed trays (those with 40 cells are best). Lettuce germinates at low temperatures so an unheated greenhouse or windowsill in a cool room will suffice.
March	Space plants 30cm apart each way. Some small varieties such as 'Little Gem' can be grown 23cm apart, and for large firm heads of crisphead varieties increase the spacing to 38cm. In a vegetable plot: sow directly into a well-raked seedbed. Make seed drills about 1.5cm deep and 30cm apart. Sow seed thinly and thin out in stages to leave one seedling every 30cm. For containers, borders and vegetable plots: sow seed in small pots. Rather than sowing lots of the same variety, try sowing a few pots of several varieties. Keep the pots or trays somewhere cool and sheltered.
April–July	Keep sowing further batches at fortnightly intervals into July to maintain a constant supply throughout the summer. Plants raised in pots: plant out as soon as they have four true leaves. In a raised bed or container: sow or plant short rows across the bed at fortnightly intervals to produce a continuous supply. Four or five lettuces a fortnight should be plenty.
August	A final sowing can be worthwhile for an autumn crop. Use a variety that is resistant to downy mildew (see page 89). Alternatively, sow a loose-leaved variety and pick leaves as required, rather than hearted lettuce. You could also plant a hardy winter lettuce, which will produce loose leaves the following spring, or hearts in May

SALAD LEAVES

These days, salad means so much more than just lettuce and cucumber. Continental salad leaves, hot oriental leaves, herbs – in fact, almost any edible leaf is now acceptable as a salad ingredient. And because you can harvest the leaves of all these plants as soon as they are large enough to pick, you can grow them in the smallest of spaces – even without a garden. Cut-and-come-again salad leaves are ideal for a window box, patio container or the smallest raised bed.

By following the instructions given here, you can have a constant supply of fresh salad leaves to rival those you can buy in the supermarket. They will not only be fresher but can be grown organically, too. As well as lettuce and oriental greens (see pages 88–91 and 96–9), you can grow a whole range of leafy plants to vary the mix each time you pick an instant salad.

Know your salad leaves

Beet leaves have a characteristic, earthy beetroot flavour.

Chervil has finely divided leaves that have a hint of aniseed. An essential ingredient if you want to perk up blander leaves.

Coriander is slow at first but is easier to grow as the weather warms

GOOD VARIETIES

Beet leaves
'Bull's Blood'
(reddest of leaves)

Rocket
'Voyager' (spicy wild rocket)

Coriander
'Calypso'(can be cut several times)

up, and good over winter. Choose a named variety for leaf rather than seed production, and sow little and often, as it tends to run to flower.

Cress can be grown successfully as a cut-and-come again crop as well as on kitchen roll.

Rocket has a unique taste that is hard to describe. At the baby leaf stage it can be subtle, but it gets hotter with age.

Salad burnet has nice-looking leaves that resemble flat-leafed parsley.

Spinach True spinach doesn't re-sprout readily from a cut stump. It's useful, however, for adding bulk with its buttery green leaves. Grow plenty, and if it gets too big, cut the whole lot and cook it.

Watercress is easy to grow in a container provided you keep it well watered and in the shade. Don't expect the large succulent leaves grown in running water, but the smaller leaves do pack a peppery punch.

# Salad Crops

HEALTH WATCH!

Bolting Some salad plants bolt, or start to flower quickly, especially in warmer weather. Rocket and pak choi, in particular, are better planted early or late in the the season.

Keep a watch for slugs and snails and aphids (see pages 40–1).

Preparing and caring

The best way to grow salad leaves is in containers or raised beds as they can otherwise be difficult to weed.

1 Take a plant pot – one at least 20cm wide and deep is best. Fill it almost to the brim with multipurpose compost and firm gently

2 Add a generous pinch of salad-leaf seeds.You can use a ready-made mixture or mix your own with your favourite ingredients. Spread the seeds as evenly as possible and not too thickly

3 Cover with a sprinkling of compost and water well. Stand the pot outside in a semi-shaded spot. Do not thin out or transplant and keep them well watered

4 For cut-and-come-again salad leaves, wait until the majority of the leaves reach 7–10cm (four to six weeks later), then cut with scissors about 2cm from the compost surface. Carefully remove all the cut leaves – any cut ones left lying around will rot

5 A week or two later the cut stumps will start to re-sprout. Wait until the new leaves reach 7–10cm and repeat.With luck, you should get three cuts from each crop

To sow the seeds in a bed, sow in bands or in single rows, 10cm apart with roughly 1–2cm between seeds.

When sowing seeds in batches, do so according to the growth of the previous batch rather than the calendar. When one batch is a week or so from its first cut, start the next one.

Plant autumn and winter salads as plants from pots or modular trays. They will stand more chance of avoiding the local slug and snail population. If frost is likely, put fleece over the salads.

Harvesting and storing

For really fresh salad, pick it at the last minute, wash thoroughly and shake dry. Pick immature plants or individual leaves as required.

SOWING AND GROWING

February	The first batch of salad leaves in containers can be started off under cover. Scatter the seed thinly and cover with a dusting of compost. Keep well watered. Move the containers outside as conditions allow. Outside: use cloches to cover seed sown directly in the ground or sow in containers and cover them with garden fleece.
March–August	Sow small amounts at regular intervals. Either sow at two- or three-week intervals and accept the later sowings will start to catch up with the earlier ones, or wait until one sowing has germinated or reached a certain stage before sowing the next batch. This should help to spread them out over the season.
September	It is worth making a final sowing of hardy salad plants, such as Chinese cabbage and other oriental greens (see pages 96–9), corn salad, endive, kale and rocket to harvest from autumn to spring. Sow in modular trays and plant outside in October. Grow under fleece to protect from frost and watch out for slug damage.

Salad Crops

GOOD VARIETIES

Chinese cabbage 'Blues'

Pak choi 'Joi Choi' (white stalks)

'Tatsoi' (green rosettes)

Mustard 'Red Frills' (red frilly leaves)

'Golden Streaks' (frilly golden leaves)

'Mizuna' (quick-growing leaf)

ORIENTAL GREENS

Despite the popularity of Chinese food, oriental greens are not widely grown in the UK. This is unfortunate, as they are a quick, easy crop and decorative enough for a small garden.

There are two main points to consider when growing these vegetables. First, they have a tendency to bolt if sown too early, but this is easily prevented by choosing improved varieties or by sowing later in the summer than European cabbages. A second potential problem is that oriental greens are prey to all the pests and diseases that affect other members of the cabbage family (see pages 153–7). So it is worth covering the crop with fine mesh.

Like European cabbages, oriental greens require a very fertile, moisture-retentive soil, with a high nitrogen content. This is particularly important if you are using them as a follow-on crop from mid-summer onwards, to enrich the soil. Crops for cut-and-come-again are best grown in containers if you don't have weed-free ground (see page 94).

Know your greens
Celtuce or Chinese stem lettuce is a type of lettuce with a tender edible stem. It is no relation of celery, but the stems have a similar mild flavour and crunchy texture. It is best as a summer-to-autumn crop. Harvest it when the stems are 30cm tall and 2.5cm thick.

Chinese broccoli or Chinese kale is grown mainly for its edible flowering shoots. It can be sown throughout the summer and crops after about two months. Modern varieties, such as 'Apollo' crossed with conventional calabrese, are worth growing as they are a quicker alternative to calabrese.

Chinese cabbage These are either tall and cylindrical or barrel-shaped. The barrel-shaped ones are best suited to the UK climate. They have a mild flavour and crunchy texture and can be used as a substitute for iceberg lettuce.

Chop suey greens or shungiku is a type of chrysanthemum that flowers very quickly. If it is sown little and often and picked young, its leaves add a piquancy to salads or can be cooked as spinach. It becomes very bitter when it starts to bolt.

Komatsuna or mustard spinach (1) can be used as a salad ingredient or, when larger, in stir-fries.

Mizuna (2) is a Japanese green and produces frilly rosettes of mild leaves. It is very vigorous but performs well as a cut-and-come-again salad.

Mibuna is similar to mizuna with rounded leaves.

Mustards These have a hotter flavour than Chinese cabbage and pak choi and are best stir-fried. The seedlings are milder and used in salads.

Pak choi (3) Even though these vegetables do not make dense hearts, the fleshy, mild-flavoured leaf stalks are edible. Upright varieties with either white or green stalks are the most commonly available. Tatsoi has flatter rosettes of green leaves.

Salad Crops

Cabbage pests that attack oriental greens include **cabbage aphid, cabbage root fly, cabbage white butterflies and clubroot** (see pages 153–6).

Flea beetle are potential pests (see page 101).

Slugs and snails relish the young tender leaves of oriental greens (see pages 40–1).

Preparing and caring

If your soil is not weed-free, grow oriental greens for salads in containers.

For large plants prepare the soil by forking in garden compost or well-rotted manure. Give the soil a thorough soaking if it is dry, and scatter a generous amount of balanced fertiliser.

Cover the crop with insect-proof netting or be prepared to hand-pick or spray pests. Water the plants well and, if possible, apply a mulch of well-rotted organic matter to help keep the roots moist.

Chinese cabbage and pak choi are not very frost-hardy, so cover later sowings in September with cloches or garden fleece. A late sowing in a greenhouse or polythene tunnel, which can be kept frost-free, should provide fresh greens all winter.

Harvesting and storing

The leaves can be cut at any stage, either as seedlings or as immature plants. Spring-sown plants are likely to bolt if left too long, though the flower shoots are also edible before the flowers open.

Cut-and-come-again
All types of oriental greens respond well to the cut-and-come-again treatment (see page 94).

Cut Chinese cabbage heads, leaving a stump – this should produce a flush of new leaves. Mature heads and older leaves are best steamed or used in stir-fries. Younger leaves, immature plants and seedlings of all oriental greens can be used as alternative salad ingredients.

SOWING AND GROWING

March–May	Sow all types of oriental greens in containers for a crop of loose leaves (see also Salad Leaves, pages 92–5). (Chinese cabbages have rough seed leaves, which are not as good to eat as when they are larger.)
June	Most oriental greens are a useful follow-on crop after broad beans or peas have finished. Chinese cabbage will bolt if transplanted from a seedbed, so sow these and other kinds of oriental greens directly into their final position and thin out later or start the seed off in 7cm pots, ready to follow an early crop. Keep them in partial shade and watch out for pests.
July	Further sowings can be made throughout July, although they will need to be kept moist. When planting, Chinese cabbage and larger types of oriental greens need a spacing of 30–38cm each way to produce heads. Pak choi can be planted as close as 23cm apart. Direct-sown crops: thin to the spacings above, or to a closer spacing of 10–15cm apart for a crop of loose greens.
August	Make a final sowing of Chinese cabbage for an autumn crop. Mature heads from the earliest sowing should be ready to harvest.

RADISHES

Summer radishes are very easy to grow and will fit into the smallest garden, or even a patio container or window box. They are quick, too, taking only four to six weeks from sowing to harvest. By sowing small amounts in succession through the summer, you can have a constant supply of radishes for adding colour and spice to salads, or as a garnish.

If you have more space, consider radish pods as an unusual border plant, or the more exotic winter radishes. These are not often grown in the UK, though they are popular in the Far East as a winter vegetable. They can grow very large, and although some milder varieties are eaten raw as a salad vegetable, others are very hot. The long white moolis found in the supermarket are a type of winter radish. Like other oriental vegetables (see pages 96–9), winter radishes are a useful follow-on crop after an earlier vegetable has been harvested, because they are best sown from July onwards.

Preparing and caring

Grow summer radishes with related crops (any member of the cabbage family) and rotate them around the vegetable plot on a three- or four-year cycle (see pages 21–3). Because flea beetles tend to hibernate in the soil under a previous crop, covering radishes with garden fleece should stop them attacking new sowings in a different area. Bear in mind that a 1m row will yield about a kilo of radishes; a 30cm pot about ten bunches.

HEALTH WATCH!

Summer radishes are in the ground for so little time that they rarely suffer problems. However, **Flea beetles** may nibble radishes and members of the cabbage family, such as rocket, kale and oriental greens, but generally do little damage. As the beetles hibernate in the soil, crop rotation combined with a covering of garden fleece should offer complete protection.

Winter radishes are especially prone to **clubroot** and **cabbage root fly,** which will both produce swollen and distorted roots (see pages 153 and 156).

For mild-flavoured, crunchy roots, summer radishes need to grow rapidly without a check to their growth. Lack of water will make them woody and hot, so in dry spells water weekly. Aim to wet the soil thoroughly rather than just sprinkle the surface.

Radish pods If you let any radish bolt, it will produce a large, sparse head of small white or purplish flowers. Leave it, and an impressive crop of hollow green pods will form. These are crunchy and slightly hot. They make an unusual edible addition to an ornamental border and will continue cropping for some time if picked regularly. Support the flower stems with sticks to prevent the plant falling over.

Harvesting and storing

Pull radishes as soon as they reach about 2cm across. Much larger than 3cm and they will start to become tough.

Winter radish roots should be large enough to harvest at some point around October when they have developed the shape and skin colour characteristic of the variety. Before this, they are likely to be hotter-flavoured and will not store.

- They can be left in the ground, but may be damaged by frost or slugs. Cover the rows with a layer of straw.
- Once mature, the roots can also be lifted and stored indoors. Cut off the leaves to within 5cm of the root; removing the leaves prevents the stored roots drying out. Stand the roots upright in a box and pack damp sand round them. Leave the tops exposed to the air to prevent rotting. In a cool but frost-free place they will keep for months.

SOWING AND GROWING

March	Make the first couple of summer radish sowings under cloches.
April–June	Sow summer radish seeds thinly in a seed drill 1cm deep and 10–15cm apart. Allow room to get a hoe between the rows for weeding. Aim for a seed about every 2.5cm, but do not bother to thin out the seedlings – the round roots will push each other apart as they grow. In pots or a window box: scatter the seed on the surface of the compost, aiming for a seed every 2.5–5cm apart each way, then cover with another 1cm of compost. Sow small batches at intervals for a continuous supply.
June	Sow winter radishes after the longest day, or they will run to seed. Sow the seed directly into open ground in seed drills 1cm deep and 25cm apart. If the soil is dry, water the drill thoroughly before sowing.
July	Thin the seedlings of winter radishes to 15cm apart, to give them plenty of room to produce large roots. They will need little attention during the summer and autumn. In milder areas, a final summer radish sowing is still worthwhile. Cover late sowings in colder areas with cloches. You could also use up spare seed in a vacant greenhouse border over winter.

GOOD VARIETIES

Celery
'Victoria' (reliable green type)

Celeriac
'Monarch' (standard variety)

Fennel
'Zefa Fino' (standard variety)

CELERY, CELERIAC AND FENNEL

Modern self-blanching varieties of celery mean that it is much easier to grow than it used to be as earthing up is no longer an important part of the growing process. Celery prefers an open site with a fertile soil that holds moisture well. If the soil is acid, you will need to add lime (see the 'Top tip' on page 27) to raise the pH to 7.0 (neutral).

Celeriac is a close relative of celery, with a thickened, edible stem base. It requires the same rich, moist soil to thrive. It prefers a cool, damp climate.

Florence fennel is a type of fennel that is bred for its fleshy stem base and the feathery foliage is a very attractive addition in the ornamental border. It has a subtle aniseed flavour and can be eaten raw, casseroled or braised.

Preparing and caring

There is no point sowing celery seeds too early; count back 10–12 weeks from the last frost date for your area. Keep the seedlings frost-free and the compost moist. Pull out any weak seedlings or those with blistered or spotted foliage and grow on the rest until they have four to six leaves.

Plant celery plants in blocks with the plants 23cm apart each way. Water the plants in well and use a cover of garden fleece overnight for the first couple of weeks. Water once to twice a week after planting. Thereafter continue to water – be prepared to apply 10 litres a sq m twice a week in dry spells – and feed the plants occasionally with a high-nitrogen fertiliser.

TRY THIS

When the swollen base of Florence fennel is plump and fleshy, cut just above soil level. The stump may produce a crop of smaller shoots. Trim the larger leaves off the 'bulb'. While it is growing, use the ferny leaves for flavouring.

Plant celeriac into their final position when they are 5–8cm high. Give each plant a space of 30cm in diameter. Water well in dry spells and give a high-nitrogen feed from time to time during the summer. Mulch between the plants with a 15cm layer of old straw or well-rotted compost to help conserve moisture. Remove the lower leaves regularly later in the summer to help the roots swell.

HEALTH WATCH!

Carrot fly can tunnel into the roots and stalks causing stunted growth and yellow foliage. There is little you can do but destroy the plant. It can be prevented by planting after mid-June (see also page 204).

Celery fly grubs tunnel into the leaves and cause them to develop yellow-brown blotches. Pick off and destroy badly affected leaves.

Leaf spot, caused by a seed-borne disease, results in brown spots on the leaves. Look out for this from the seedling stage and destroy affected plants. Most celery seed is treated to prevent leaf spot.

Mosaic virus, a disease that is spread by aphids (see page 78).

Slugs like celery plants (see pages 40–1).

Bolting celery plants is a common problem in dry summers. The secret is to keep the plants growing steadily from the seedling stage onwards. So do not let them go short of water or wait in their pots too long before being transplanted. Self-blanching varieties are less prone to bolting than the old-fashioned trench varieties.

Florence fennel prefers a Mediterranean climate, growing best in a warm site in light, well-drained soil. Work in plenty of well-rotted organic matter and water in very dry spells. Florence fennel dislikes being planted out when it is larger (i.e. once a rootball has formed), but it grows very rapidly, producing a 'bulb' in 10–12 weeks. When the stem base starts to swell, you can pile up soil around the stem to make it whiter, although this is not essential. In the UK climate, it is best to sow in late June. It is liable to bolt if sown too early or in a cold summer.

Harvesting and storing

To harvest celery, remove any straw or earth from around the plants. Ease a garden fork down into the ground and lift the celery plant out. Cut off the roots and discard any damaged outer stems. Replace any straw or earth around nearby plants. Any surplus can be lifted and stored in a cool, frost-free place for several weeks.

To prevent celeriac rotting, pull off all the leaf stalks except the innermost tuft. Store celeriac in boxes of moist sand during the winter until needed. However, the flavour is likely to be better if they are left in the ground. Cover them with straw or dried bracken to protect them from severe frosts, and use slug pellets if slugs are a problem.

SOWING AND GROWING

February–March	Sow celeriac seed in seed trays in gentle heat (12°C or less), then grow on in a greenhouse. The seed needs light to germinate so scatter it on the compost surface and do not cover it. Keep the compost moist by covering the trays with a sheet of glass. Germination may be slow and erratic. Prick out the seedlings into small pots or modular seed trays when they are large enough to handle easily.
March–April	Start celery seeds in a greenhouse or somewhere you can maintain a temperature of 15°C. Use a seed tray or a modular tray. Sow the seeds on the surface of the compost. Cover them lightly with vermiculite or place a sheet of glass on top of the tray. Mist the seeds with a hand-held spray; they should germinate after about two weeks. Get celery and celeriac plants used to outdoor conditions gradually by hardening them off (see page 63). For a summer crop, sow a couple of Florence fennel seeds per 7cm pot and start off in a greenhouse. Transplant the young seedlings when they have two pairs of leaves, 30cm apart.
May–June	If you forgot to sow celery seeds, buy celery plants instead. Prior to planting, rake in a general fertiliser. Plant out celeriac plants in May.
June–July	For autumn crops, sow Florence fennel seed directly into a well-prepared seedbed and water thoroughly if the soil is dry. Germination can be erratic, but the seedlings will not suffer a check to their growth by being transplanted. Thin to 30cm apart.
August	Start harvesting celery plants on the outside of the block first. Straw can be tucked in between the remaining plants to enhance blanching.
September	Continue to harvest celery and Florence fennel as required.
October	Aim to finish harvesting celery and Florence fennel before the frosts, but celeriac is best kept in the ground (see above).

GOOD VARIETIES

Spinach
'Mikado'

Chard
'Bright Lights'
(colourful mixture)

SPINACH AND CHARD

True spinach is an annual, green leafy plant. Better known as a cooked vegetable, the young leaves, or baby spinach, are also used raw in salads.

Leaf beet, or perpetual spinach, is much easier to grow than true spinach. The related chards have larger, often brightly coloured, leaf stalks that make striking ornamental plants for containers or borders. Further afield, most parts of the world have different crops cooked as a spinach, many of which you can try in your garden.

As it is an annual, true spinach will bolt or run to seed in the first season. To avoid this, it is therefore best sown in succession through the summer and cut when small, before it starts to bolt.

Preparing and caring

It is easiest to sow spinach directly into a well-prepared seedbed. Rake in some balanced fertiliser and water if the soil is dry. Start the first couple of sowings under cloches in cold areas. Spinach is a useful catch crop (see page 52).

Keep picking all leaves over regularly. Leaf beet and chard that has been picked over regularly will benefit from a scattering of high-nitrogen fertiliser to boost further leaf production.

HEALTH WATCH!

True spinach and leaf beet are generally trouble free, though they may be attacked by **aphids** (see page 41) or downy mildew (see page 89).

Leaf miner burrows in the leaves making transparent patches. Remove badly affected leaves.

Water spinach throughout the summer by giving the soil a thorough soak once a week to prevent plants from bolting. In cold areas in autumn, protect true spinach with cloches.

Leaf beets, including the coloured-stemmed chards, are biennials and are less likely to bolt in the first summer. They are best sown once in spring and the leaves harvested regularly.

Harvesting and storing

True spinach is usually cut when it reaches a certain size and will not regrow. Pick when leaves are 5–10cm for eating raw in salads. For cooking, let it grow to 15–20cm. You need to collect a large amount of leaves, as they condense hugely in the cooking process.

Leaf beet grows very fast, producing large leaves. Pick the outer leaves regularly when they reach 10–15cm, allowing the central leaves to continue growing. You can also cut the whole head about 2cm above soil level. The plant should re-sprout. Leaf beet will continue growing all summer and can be picked over regularly. Older, larger leaves can be cooked, but remember to strip out the tough midribs first.

Pick chard leaves when they are very small for salads or cook them like leaf beet. The leaf stalks are also edible. They can be cooked with the leaves when small. Larger stalks are best separated from the leaf and steamed or boiled as a separate dish. The coloured-stemmed types are particularly appealing.

Spring-sown leaf beet and chard should survive over winter and they will provide a couple of pickings in spring and early summer before bolting.

SOWING AND GROWING

March	Make the first sowing of true spinach. Sow thinly into seed drills 1cm deep and 30cm apart. Sow short rows or small patches at a time once every three weeks to ensure a continuous crop.
April	Continue to sow small amounts of true spinach at intervals. Thin the seedlings from earlier sowings to about 10–15cm apart. These can be used in salads. Make one sowing of leaf beet. Start the seed in 7cm pots for planting out later, or sow directly into the vegetable plot. Sow into seed drills 1.5cm deep and 30cm apart. Thin the seedlings later so they are 30cm apart. Chard may bolt prematurely in the first summer if sown too early, so wait until April. In containers: aim for about six plants in a 10-litre pot, or grow individual plants in a 4-litre pot. Each seed produces a clump of seedlings, which can be thinned out later.
May	The earliest sowings of true spinach should be ready for cutting about 10–12 weeks from sowing. It is worth continuing to sow through May, but after that, the weather is likely to be too hot and the soil too dry, and plants will bolt readily.
June	Sow a variety of winter-hardy spinach for an early crop next spring. You can make a second sowing of leaf beet for picking in winter. This late sowing should continue cropping well into the following summer before bolting.
July	Keep cutting true spinach and picking over leaf beets.

CUCUMBERS

Summer would not be the same without cucumber for sandwiches and salads. If you have a greenhouse, cucumbers are fairly easy to grow, and a couple of plants will reward you with a constant supply of fresh fruits. If you have a sunny, sheltered spot on the patio, some greenhouse varieties are worth trying outdoors, too. Follow the growing instructions for greenhouse cucumbers (see page 114) and plant outside after the last frost has passed; or grow an outdoor or ridge cucumber in a large container. The trailing varieties can be trained up a wigwam or a trellis.

You can grow cucumbers from seed, but ready-grown plants are widely available in garden centres and are easier to look after if you do not heat your greenhouse earlier in the spring.

Preparing and caring

Heat your greenhouse You will need a heated propagator to maintain a minimum temperature of 25°C for the seeds to germinate, and somewhere warm to grow the young plants on. You can alternatively germinate them in an airing cupboard, but transfer them to a warm, well-lit windowsill as soon as the seedlings emerge.

Cucumbers are vulnerable to soil rots, so it is best to grow them in growing bags or pots filled with multipurpose compost. Plant two plants to a standard growing bag, or one plant to a 15-litre pot. If you choose to grow them in the greenhouse border, change the position each year, alternating with tomatoes to prevent diseases building up.

GOOD VARIETIES

Indoors
'Flamingo' (for full-size)

'Passandra' (for half-sized fruits)

Outdoors
'Green Fingers' (snack-sized fruits)

'Rocky' (snack-sized fruits)

cucumbers

HEALTH WATCH!

Spider mites are hard to see with the naked eye, but inspect the undersides of the leaves regularly for the characteristic flecking and webbing. They can build up rapidly. A severe infestation will result in masses of fine webbing and the leaves will start to yellow and die. Spray with an insecticide based on pyrethrum, which is the only option if outdoor cucumbers are attacked. In the greenhouse you can also use biological control (see page 43). To help control them, keep the greenhouse humid by regularly damping down the paths.

As the plants grow, gradually increase the watering. If possible, use water at greenhouse temperature, rather than straight from the tap. To save time make a mini-reservoir for each plant out of a plastic drink bottle. Cut off the base and make a small hole in the cap. Push the bottle cap-end first into the compost and fill with water. The water will seep out over a couple of hours.

Outdoor bush or climbing varieties need a container that can hold 30 litres of compost. In the garden, unless the soil is already very rich, prepare a planting hole. Dig a hole 30cm in diameter and 30cm deep. Fill this with a mixture of soil and well-rotted manure or garden compost. Replace the surplus soil to leave a low mound. Plant into the top of this mound to help prevent stem rot. Allow a space of at least 75cm in diameter for bush or trailing varieties, or 45cm if they are to grow up supports.

In the greenhouse, train each plant up a single cane or string. Wind the young shoot round the support, tying in if necessary. Remove the flower buds, tendrils and side shoots from the first 45cm of stem, leaving just one leaf at each joint. After this, keep removing any side shoots, but allow the flower buds to develop. Keep doing this until the leading shoot reaches the top of the support.

HEALTH WATCH!

Powdery mildew manifests as white powdery patches across the leaves of indoor cucumbers (see page 122). Regular watering, but avoid wetting the leaves, and correct spacing of plants to prevent overcrowding will help to offset mildew. If you are growing cucumbers in a greenhouse, open the vents on hot days and give the plants plenty of room. Remove and destroy any infected debris to prevent the fungus overwintering. Some varieties have some resistance to mildew.

Whitefly settle on the undersides of leaves and make them sticky and encourage a black mould to grow (see aphids on page 41). A biological control for whitefly in the greenhouse is also available (see page 43).

In a border you can train them up wigwams or tripods of canes or bean sticks, about 1.5m tall. Or train them up trellis or on wires on a sunny fence. An alternative approach in a border is to plant them on the flat and mulch generously with composted bark or compost. This will help suppress weeds and conserve soil moisture. Leave a gap of a couple of centimetres around the stem to prevent stem rot.

When climbing plants reach the top of the support, pinch out the tip to encourage side shoots. Similarly, when trailing plants have six or seven large leaves, pinch out the growing tip. Bush varieties need no such treatment. Outdoor varieties do not need training like greenhouse types.

SOWING AND GROWING GREENHOUSE CUCUMBERS

March	If you start to heat your greenhouse through the spring, sow the seed in March (see page 111), otherwise wait until April.
April	Sow the seed now if you do not heat your greenhouse. Sow seed singly in 7cm pots containing multipurpose compost. Seed of the all-female hybrid varieties is very expensive, so use enough to raise a couple of plants and store the surplus seed for next year. Cucumber seeds should germinate in about three days under ideal conditions. Pot them on into a larger pot (12cm is ideal), as soon as the first leaves have fully opened. This avoids disturbing the roots by potting on several times.
May	About four weeks later, when the young plants have four or five leaves, they should be ready to plant out. But wait until early June if the greenhouse is unheated. Harden them off carefully if you have raised them indoors (see page 63). Do not buy cucumber plants too early, unless you have somewhere warm to keep them.
June	Plant out in an unheated greenhouse in colder areas. Keep watering to a minimum and water only in the morning to avoid wet soil overnight. It is easy to overwater cucumber plants at this stage. Cut slits in the growing bags near the base to drain off excess water. Cucumbers prefer a temperature of at least 21°C. If you have automatic greenhouse vent openers, set them to this temperature. Start training the plants (see page 113).
July–August	Growing bag compost should contain sufficient nutrients for about four weeks. Once the first fruits start to form, feed regularly with a tomato feed. Pick off dead or yellowing leaves from the base of the plant.

Harvesting and storing

Once a cucumber fruit has reached a decent size (around 30cm for a normal-sized variety; 15cm for a half-sized one and 10cm for a bite-sized one), cut it off and store in a cool place. Even if you cannot eat them all, pick mature fruit or further flowering and fruit initiation will cease.

Outdoor varieties are generally shorter and fatter than greenhouse varieties. The older varieties in particular have rough or spiny skins, and contain immature seeds. Pick the fruits regularly, even if you cannot eat them, or further cropping will cease.

SOWING AND GROWING CUCUMBERS OUTDOORS

April	Start the seeds in pots somewhere warm. Sow two or three per 7cm pot about 1cm deep in good multipurpose compost. Keep them at a constant 18–21°C until the seedlings appear. If more than one comes up, pull out the weaker one. Grow them on at around 15°C and keep the compost moist, but do not overwater.
May	They will grow rapidly, but cannot be planted outdoors until all danger of frost has passed. If necessary, pot them into large pots to prevent a check to growth. In mild areas it should be safe to plant out in late May, but in colder areas, wait until early or mid-June.
June	The plants can now be planted outside (see page 112).
July	Water the plants regularly. Give them a watering-can-full twice a week in dry weather. When the first fruits start to swell, use a tomato feed once a week. Do not remove male flowers of outdoor cucumbers (the ones with no bump at their base), because pollination is necessary to produce fruits.
August	Start to pick fruits when they reach 15–20cm in length.

ASPARAGUS

Asparagus is a luxury vegetable that is not hard to grow but does need patience. A decent-sized bed (one that contains at least ten plants) takes up a lot of space. If you have room for only a couple of plants, grow them at the back of a border to provide a feathery foil for other plants during summer.

Once established, asparagus will crop year after year with little effort, other than a mulch of organic matter. The fresh spears taste delicious when cooked straight from the garden.

Preparing and caring

Establish a new bed or plant in a border in early April. As a very rough guide, ten established plants should yield about 3kg of spears over a six-week period each year for up to 20 years. Don't pick the spears for the first two years after planting to allow the asparagus time to become established.

- The simplest way to start a bed is to buy crowns in April. Crowns are the dormant bases of one-year-old plants. The ideal site is well drained, with neutral or slightly alkaline soil and free of perennial weeds. If necessary, create a raised bed.
- Dig in plenty of well-rotted organic matter – spent mushroom compost is ideal. Allow 45cm between plants and 90cm between rows.
- Dig a trench or a hole wide enough to spread out the roots of the crowns. Lay the crowns gently on to a ridge or mound in the centre of the trench or hole with the roots spread on either side. The top of the crown should be 10–13cm below the soil surface. Cover with loose soil.

On established beds, scatter a balanced fertiliser in March or mulch with well-rotted organic matter, which also helps to prevent weeds.

- The first spears should be ready in late April on established plants.

- Stop cutting spears on two-year-old plants in May to allow the ferns to develop and build up the plants' underground reserves for the following season.
- Stop cutting established plants towards the middle of June and apply a high-nitrogen fertiliser to encourage the ferns.
- Weed by hand to prevent weeds, especially perennials, gaining a foothold. In exposed areas, vigorously growing ferns may need some support with canes and string.

Harvesting and storing

Cut the spears about 2.5–5cm below the soil with a sharp knife. The white base can be trimmed off or used as a handle when eating. Spears should be at least 10cm long with a tight bud. Check twice a week, as they can grow very rapidly.

It may be necessary to store spears until you accumulate sufficient for a meal.

Asparagus also freezes well, if you are lucky enough to have a surplus. Blanch spears for 2–4 minutes, depending on their size.

SOWING AND GROWING

April	Plant new crowns (see opposite). Start to harvest the spears from established plants when they reach 15–20cm.
May	Stop cutting spears from plants in their first year.
June	Stop cutting spears in their second year onwards in mid–late June.
October	Cut down the dead ferns, remove weeds and mulch with organic matter.

THE SQUASH FAMILY

Courgettes are a must-have crop, producing a constant supply of tasty fruits all summer. But don't just confine yourself to courgettes. The squash family includes lots of interesting alternatives. Summer squash come in a range of shapes and colours, and winter squash store right through the year – ideal for winter soups and roasts. If you have kids who love Halloween, a pumpkin or two becomes essential growing, too.

The Squash Family

GOOD VARIETIES

Courgettes
'Defender' (standard green)

'Parthenon' (self-setting green fruits)

'Soleil' (yellow)

Marrow
'Bush Baby' (striped courgette or small marrow)

COURGETTES, SUMMER SQUASH AND MARROWS

Courgette plants can take up a lot of space, spreading at least 1m across. But if you can find room for them in a border or a patio tub, you will be rewarded with a constant supply of tender courgettes throughout the summer months. The large, silvery-flecked leaves and bright-yellow flowers are attractive, too. There are some compact varieties for containers.

Summer squash have soft skins. Treat them like courgettes and pick when young.

Do not make the mistake of growing a marrow variety and picking the fruits when they are still small. It is much better to start with a variety bred specifically for courgette production, or the total number of fruits may be disappointing.

If you are growing marrows, there is a choice of bush or trailing varieties to be had. If you find marrows bland, consider winter squash, which are just as easy to grow (see pages 125–7).

Preparing and caring

Courgettes and summer squash are very sensitive to frost, so it is not worth planting them outside until all risk has passed. In most areas, this means waiting until early to mid-June. They are, however, very fast-growing plants. In very mild parts, and if you can provide a sheltered, sunny position, you could sow directly outdoors. But it is simpler to sow the seed in pots in a greenhouse or on a warm windowsill for planting out in June.

Prepare a planting hole unless the soil is already rich in organic matter. Dig a hole up to 30cm wide and deep. Refill with a mixture of soil and well-rotted manure or garden compost. This will leave a low mound. Water both the hole and the plant well and plant into the top of the mound. This will direct excess rain away from the base of the plant and help to prevent stem rot.

5 MINUTE JOB

To help with watering, try burying a length of plastic drainpipe, or a large plastic bottle with the bottom cut off, about 20cm from each plant to direct water to the roots. This is especially worthwhile if you applied a mulch earlier.

courgettes, summer squash and marrows

The Squash Family

The best way to prevent weeds later in the summer is to cover the area with permeable plastic mulch before planting out. Cut cross-shaped slits in the plastic and plant through them. Alternatively, mulch the soil around each plant with well-rotted manure, chipped bark or garden compost to suppress weeds and conserve moisture.

Allow an area at least 1m in diameter for each plant. Although the plants grow as a bush, they tend to go in one direction, so give them plenty of room to avoid swamping neighbouring plants.

To grow a courgette plant in a container you will need one that can hold at least 30 litres of compost (or the contents of a standard growing bag). You will also need to water and feed regularly (see July). Water sparingly at first, aiming to keep the soil moist. Do not overwater or you will simply encourage too much leaf.

Hand pollinating Early in the season or in cold, windy periods, pollinating insects may be scarce and fruits may not set. If this happens, you can hand-pollinate the female flowers – those with a swelling at the base. Pick a male flower (with a straight stem and no swelling), remove its petals and gently push it into the female flower.

For an early crop in a greenhouse use a self-fertile variety such as 'Parthenon', whch does not require insect pollinators.

TIP
Feed plants, especially those in containers, with a dilute tomato feed once a week.

Harvesting and storing

Check fruits at least twice a week and pick courgettes when they reach 15cm. For marrows, pick them when they reach 25–30cm in length. If you are going away for a couple of weeks, remove all of the flowers and fruits, to prolong cropping.

⊷€ The Squash Family

To store marrows over winter, gather the mature fruits before the first severe frost. Often the first mild frost of the autumn will cause the foliage to collapse and make harvesting easier. Do not leave it too late, or the fruits will be harmed too.

Store only sound, fully ripened marrows with hard skins. They should keep for up to four months, given suitable conditions. Stand them in a single layer, not touching, on wooden trays. Better still, hang them individually in nets to allow air to circulate around them. Store in a well-ventilated, cool (but frost-free) shed or outbuilding. Check occasionally for any signs of rotting.

SOWING AND GROWING

May	Sow the seeds on edge and singly into 7cm pots and cover with compost. Two courgette plants should be plenty for most families; expect up to 30 fruits from each. Given a minimum temperature of 18°C, plants germinate and grow very rapidly. Keep them well watered and if you cannot plant them out within four weeks, pot them on into bigger pots. Gradually harden them off (see page 63).
June	It should be safe to plant out in mid-June in all but the coldest areas. Delay until later in the month if there is any chance of a late frost.
July–August	Once flowering starts, a good soaking once a week will be more effective in dry weather than regular light watering. Pick fruits regularly to encourage further cropping.
September–October	Most varieties will continue cropping until the first frost. Leave marrow fruits to ripen and develop their full colour. Striped varieties will turn green and yellow and harden.

PUMPKINS AND WINTER SQUASH

Pumpkins are a familiar sight at Halloween, hollowed out and carved into lanterns, but their flesh can be disappointingly lacking in flavour. Some smaller varieties of pumpkin, such as 'Baby Bear', however, are an excellent choice for eating.

When it comes to winter squash, a huge range of shapes and sizes is available. Most are vigorous, trailing plants, which need a lot of space – each plant can give up to eight fruits, depending on the variety, weighing up to 10kg a plant, though those with smaller fruits can be trained up trellis and arches. Unlike pumpkins, winter squash will store well into the New Year. Some are very decorative, and most have a rich, nutty or buttery taste, ideal for hearty winter soups and stews.

GOOD VARIETIES

Pumpkin 'Charmant' (tidy plants, medium fruit)

Squash 'Crown Prince' (reliable, large fruits)

'Harrier' (butternut for UK gardens)

'Uchiki Kuri' (small and tasty)

pumpkins and winter squash

The Squash Family

Preparing and caring

Pumpkins and winter squash are very sensitive to frost and need a long, hot summer to ripen fully. Grow them exactly as you would marrows (see pages 121–4).

Once established, they are very easy going. They will crop even in a dry year, though a couple of really thorough soakings when the fruits are swelling will increase the crop.

They can be rampant trailers. Keep them relatively neat by training the main shoots in a circle. Alternatively, plant next to sweetcorn and let the squash use the space under the corn stems.

Harvesting and storing

Pumpkins and winter squash should be ripening nicely by October and the foliage will be dying down – the first autumn frost will finish it off. If the weather is cool and wet, move the fruits into the greenhouse or a sunny windowsill to finish ripening so they store well. Pumpkins won't keep much beyond Halloween, so use these first. Winter squash should keep until early spring. Cure them by keeping them in a warm room for two weeks, then somewhere dry and cool but frost-free.

SOWING AND GROWING

April	Sow the seed at a background temperature of 18–22°C. Follow the advice for growing courgettes, summer squash and marrows (see page 124). As the young seedling germinates it needs to push the whole seed out of the compost, otherwise it will rot.
May–June	Plant outside into a well-prepared planting hole after all danger of frost has passed. Allow at least 1 sq m per plant.
July–September	If shoots stray out of their allotted area, curl them round the centre of the plant. Plants trained to grow up supports should scramble on their own, but you may need to support the heavier fruits to prevent damage to the stems. If the weather is very dry, give a couple of generous soaks of water once the fruits have started to swell.
September–October	Cut and remove the full-sized fruit with the fruit stalk intact, preferably by cutting the stem on either side of it. This prevents the fruit rotting.

SUN-LOVING VEGETABLES

Nothing compares to sun-ripened tomatoes and their relatives – aubergines and peppers – picked fresh from the garden or allotment in late summer. Add delicious sweetcorn and artichokes to your plans for the ultimate mix of Mediterranean vegetables. If you haven't got a greenhouse or polytunnel, growing these popular vegetables and savoury fruits can be risky in a poor summer, but if you have the space, why not give them a go?

GOOD VARIETIES

Greenhouse
'Gardener's Delight' (favourite cherry variety)

'Shirley' (reliable salad type)

'Sioux' (tastiest in our trial)

Outdoors
'Losetto' (best blight resistance)

'Orkado' (tastiest outdoor cordon)

'Red Alert' (early bush variety)

'Tumbler' (best for baskets)

TRY THIS

If the young plants are tall and leggy, remove the lower leaves and plant them as deep as the new pot will allow. This will not harm the plant – in fact, the buried stem will quickly produce roots. Very leggy plants can be rescued by coiling the stem and burying it.

TOMATOES

If you have a greenhouse, this is the obvious place to grow tomatoes, however any garden should have room for a couple of tomato plants as well. Growing them in a greenhouse means you can give them a longer season and are likely to get bigger crops than if you grow them outdoors and they are less likely to suffer from blight disease. You can cut out the seed stage and buy young plants from a garden centre later in the spring, but raising your own plants from seed is easy and you'll have a much larger choice of varieties.

Compact varieties will grow in a container on the patio, in a window box or even in a hanging basket. Cordon tomatoes can be trained up a fence or trellis or grown on wigwams in the ornamental border. You have the choice of huge beefsteak, standard-sized plum or cherry tomatoes. Bush types need no training.

Preparing and caring

All seeds sown usually germinate, and as seed of modern hybrids can be very expensive, decide how many plants you want and sow just enough. Surplus seed can be saved and should remain viable for up to five years if stored somewhere cool and dry. An airtight jar containing a bag of silica gel, and kept in the fridge, is ideal.

Work plenty of organic matter into the soil in a greenhouse border or outside before planting to provide nutrients and retain moisture. If you do not have borders, or have had poor results, use large pots filled with multipurpose compost or the contents of growing bags, rather than planting in the growing bags themselves. Plant one plant to a 10-litre pot or three plants to a standard growing bag. Using 15-litre pots or two plants to a growing bag will make watering easier in high summer.

Most greenhouse tomato **varieties** are grown as cordons – tall plants with a main shoot that grows upwards for several metres. The best way to train them is to support the main stem and remove the side shoots. Bury a length of soft string under the tomato plant and attach the other end to the greenhouse frame. Or, better still, grow each plant next to a garden cane tied to the top of the greenhouse. Allow about 45cm between plants.

Repot greenhouse tomatoes when they outgrow their pots.

HEALTH WATCH!

Aphids, spider mites and whitefly can all attack greenhouse tomato leaves (see page 43 for control measures).

Blossom end rot – a sunken dark patch on the fruit – caused by inadequate watering early in the fruits' development. Later trusses should not be affected.

Flowers dropping without setting fruits or undersized fruits can be due to dry air or dryness at the roots.

Greenback – yellow patches on the shoulder of the fruit – is caused by heat injury from direct sunlight, very high temperatures or insufficient potash. Older varieties are more susceptible.

Potato blight can also attack tomatoes, especially outdoors (see page 200).

Uneven ripening can also be due to insufficient potash, lack of moisture or excessive heat.

Cont. on page 132

tomatoes

HEALTH WATCH!

Cont. from page 131

Many soil rots can affect tomato plants. Rotate crops around the greenhouse borders and thoroughly clean the greenhouse at the end of the season, to help prevent trouble. If all else fails, switch to growing in containers.

Water indoor plants frequently, which may mean twice a day in growing bags or pots on the warmest days. A trickle irrigation system will automate the process if you are not able to attend to the plants twice a day. Feed plants regularly with tomato food, and ventilate the greenhouse on sunny days – open the door as well as the roof vents.

Plant outdoor tomatoes through a black plastic mulch or add a mulch around the plants to help suppress weeds and conserve moisture in the soil. Sink a large plastic bottle, with its bottom cut off, into the soil, to act as a water reservoir and help direct water to the roots. Throughout the summer water plants regularly and feed with a liquid tomato food. Remove any dead leaves from the bottom of the plant to help the fruits ripen. Keep a lookout for signs of blight disease and aphids (see page 131).

By providing the following ideal conditions, you should experience few problems with your tomatoes:

- Water frequently in very hot spells.
- Feed regularly with a high-potash tomato fertiliser – one containing magnesium is best.
- Ventilate the greenhouse in the hottest part of the summer.
- Prevent wide fluctuations in temperature, especially at night, early in the summer.
- Keep a moist atmosphere by damping down the greenhouse floor.
- Try to keep the foliage dry to deter blight disease.

Harvesting and storing

For the best flavour, leave the fruits to ripen fully on the plant. Excess tomatoes can be frozen whole or puréed for winter use. Green tomatoes can either be encouraged to ripen by putting them in a bag with some ripe tomatoes, or made into chutney.

SOWING AND GROWING TOMATOES OUTDOORS

March–April	Start the seed off indoors or in a greenhouse about eight weeks before it is safe to plant outdoors in your area. In colder areas, wait until April.
May	In milder parts of the UK, plant outside in containers or into prepared soil in late May. Use a container with a capacity of at least 10 litres for each plant. Cover plants with fleece to protect them from cold winds, until they are well established. In colder areas or if the weather is not yet warm enough, re-pot young plants that you cannot plant outside into larger pots to prevent a check to growth.
June	Plant outside in colder areas as soon as conditions are suitable. Covering the ground with clear polythene or cloches will help to warm up the soil first. Bush varieties can be left to their own devices. Cordon varieties should be trained up a stout post up to 1.5m tall (see page 131).
October	Remove any full-sized fruit, before the plants are killed by the first frost.

Sun-loving Vegetables

SOWING AND GROWING TOMATOES INDOORS

February	If you can provide background heat in the greenhouse later in the spring, start sowing now. Plants will be ready to plant out about eight weeks from sowing.
March	Whether growing your seed for indoor or outdoor planting, scatter the seed thinly into a small pot containing moist multipurpose compost and cover with another 1cm of compost. Place the pot in a propagator set at 15–21°C. Germination takes 7–10 days; less at the higher temperature. If you do not have a propagator, cover the pot with polythene or cling film and put it in a warm place until the seedlings appear. Move them somewhere warm and light, such as on a sunny windowsill.
Early April	When the seedlings are large enough to handle, carefully separate them, holding the tip of the seed leaf, not the stem. Pot them individually into 7cm pots. Water thoroughly and keep at 18°C for a couple of days, then lower the temperature to 15°C to produce short, stocky plants. Three or four weeks after pricking out, pot the plants into 10cm pots.
Late April–May	Gradually harden off the young plants (see page 63). If you grow them on a windowsill, they may become a little leggy – turn them daily to ensure that they grow straight.
May	Plant into the open greenhouse. If you have soil borders, this is the best place to grow tomato plants. But do not grow tomatoes continuously in the same border because soil diseases gradually build up. Alternate tomatoes with non-related crops, such as cucumbers, each season.
June	Tie the main stem loosely to the support as it grows. Pinch out any side shoots that form but take care not to damage the tiny clusters of yellow flowers.
July–August	Pick the fruit when it is fully ripe and has developed its full colour.
September	Stop the plant in early September, by pinching out the growing tip of the lead shoot. This stops further trusses of fruit developing and allows the trusses already formed to ripen. Keep pinching out side shoots, and remove dead or yellowing leaves. Banana skins in the greenhouse will encourage ripening of green fruit.
October	Pick unripe fruit, clear the plants and clean the greenhouse.

PEPPERS AND CHILLIES

If you are successful with tomatoes, try growing peppers, too. You can grow different shapes and colours of sweet pepper, and also try one of the hundreds of varieties of hot chilli peppers – used to add heat to curries and other exotic dishes.

Both sweet peppers and chillies can be trained easily into neat, bushy plants and yield enough ripe fruits to more than pay for a prime site in a container on the patio. Chilli plants are particularly decorative, and just one plant should keep even the keenest chilli-eater supplied throughout the winter. In a greenhouse, both types will grow happily with the tomatoes.

Chillies
'Aurora' (good patio variety)

'Basket of Fire' (good patio variety)

Sweet peppers
'Magno' (grafted variety, orange fruit)

'Orange Bell' (small orange fruits for outdoors)

Aphids can infect greenhouse plants with a virus as well as weakening them by feeding on the sap (see page 41).

Blossom end rot can affect sweet peppers (see page 131).

Spider mites are hard to see with the naked eye, but inspect the undersides of the leaves regularly (see page 112).

Preparing and caring

When the plants reach about 20cm high, pinch out the growing tip with your finger and thumb to encourage them to branch and bush out. Vigorous varieties may require further pinching to keep them bushy.

Sweet pepper plants can be planted directly into a greenhouse border or growing bags or well-prepared beds, inside or out, and trained as cordons in the same way as tomatoes (see page 131). However, most are best grown as bushes. Remove the first fruit that forms, to encourage branching and further fruits to develop.

As the fruits start to swell you may need to water the plants twice a day on hot days. After the first flowers start to form, feed regularly with a tomato fertiliser, according to the manufacturer's instructions. It is also worth moving the plants out of a greenhouse to a sunny position outside.

Harvesting and storing

Pick peppers and chillies when they are ripe but while the skin is still smooth – avoid those with wrinkled skins. Fruits store well and will keep for up to ten days in the fridge.

Surplus chillies can be stored by drying or freezing. In tropical countries, ripe chillies are dried in the sun, but in the UK climate it is much harder to dry them completely. The long, slim types with thin walls are best for drying. It is also possible to dry chillies in an oven on the lowest setting for 24 hours or more.

SOWING AND GROWING

March	Sow two seeds to a 9cm pot. You will need a heated propagator or at least a warm windowsill, where you can maintain a constant temperature of 20°C.
April	Gradually wean the seedlings, reducing the temperature to a minimum of 14°C at night. If both seeds germinate, remove the weaker one.
May	As the plants begin to fill their small pots, pot them on into 2-litre pots of multipurpose compost (or growing bag compost).
June	Pot the plants on into 5-litre pots. This final pot should be sufficient to produce neat, manageable plants. Alternatively, plant them outside in well-prepared beds
July–August	Sweet peppers may need some support once the fruits start to swell, but chillies should look after themselves.
September	Peppers are sensitive to frost. If the fruits are still developing, move outdoor plants under cover at night.

GOOD VARIETIES

'Black Beauty' (large black variety)

'Calliope' (egg-shaped purple)

'Falcon' (large black variety)

'Ophelia' (egg-shaped black)

'Orlando' (black finger type)

AUBERGINES

Although we now know them by their French name, aubergines were originally called eggplants – some varieties are still available with round white fruits. It is not easy to grow them in the British climate, but you are more likely to succeed if you live in southern Britain, or if you have a greenhouse or polythene tunnel.

Preparing and caring

Garden centres are likely to stock a few conventional varieties, but look to the specialist vegetable catalogues for a huge choice of exotic types – purple, green, white and striped oval, round and sausage shaped.

You will need a heated propagator or at least a warm windowsill, where you can maintain a constant temperature of 20°C for germinating the seeds.

Aubergines can be difficult to grow outdoors, but if you have spare plants from the greenhouse, plant them outside. If it's still a bit cold, plant them under a cloche.

You may need to water the plants twice a day on hot days. After the first flowers start to form, feed regularly with a tomato fertiliser, according to the manufacturer's instructions. It is also worth moving the plants out of a greenhouse to a sunny position outside.

In high summer, stand the plants on a patio so that you can appreciate their attractive leaves and flowers.

Harvesting and storing
Pick fruits when they reach full size and have developed their rich purple colour.

SOWING AND GROWING

March	Sow two seeds per 9cm pot and if both seeds germinate, remove the weaker ones.
April	Gradually wean the seedlings, reducing the temperature to a minimum of 14°C at night.
May	If you have not raised plants from seed, buy small plants from a garden centre and pot into larger pots. As the plants begin to fill their small pots, pot them on into 2-litre pots of multipurpose or growing bag compost and then, by June, pot the plants on into 5-litre pots. This size pot should be sufficient to produce neat, manageable plants.
June	When the plants reach about 20cm high, pinch out the growing tip to encourage them to branch. Vigorous varieties may require further pinching to keep them bushy. Aubergines can also be planted directly into a greenhouse border or three to a growing bag. Remove the first flower that forms to encourage further flowers – and fruits.
July–August	Use split canes, if necessary, to support the main stem and each main branch, before the fruit starts to swell.
September	Aubergines are very sensitive to frost. If the fruits are still developing, move outdoor plants under cover at night.

SWEETCORN

Nothing beats the taste of fresh sweetcorn, so if you have space in your garden it is well worth growing your own. You do not need a huge vegetable plot – a group of nine plants will take up only a square metre of space and should produce at least nine cobs.

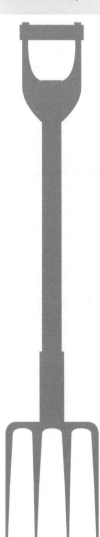

GOOD VARIETIES

'Lark' (early and very sweet)

'Swift' (reliable extra-tender variety)

'Mirai' (bicolour yellow/white cobs)

'Mirai' 003Y (child-sized sweet cobs)

Badgers, deer and pheasants can be a problem in rural areas.

Boron deficiency shows up as undeveloped cobs, dead growing tips and white-striped foliage. To prevent, apply borax at 3g a sq m when planting.

Frit fly The maggots damage the growing point and cause the plant to wilt and die in May or June. Plants are immune once they have five or six leaves. To prevent the problem, raise seedlings in pots, transplant later than normal and grow under a cover.

Mice may nibble the seed, particularly when it is sown straight into the ground. Set mousetraps or cover seeds with upturned jam jars.

Smut is a fungal disease that can infect sweetcorn. Large green or white swellings form on the developing cobs. Destroy these before they burst and spread their spores. As a precaution, grow sweetcorn on a new site next year.

Preparing and caring

Sweetcorn needs a favourable position, in full sun, as it is tender and needs a long growing season. A sheltered site will protect the tall plants from being blown over or damaged by heavy rain.

Any reasonable soil will do but avoid extremely wet or dry. The roots go deep into the soil, so dig the area over well and add plenty of well-rotted organic matter.

It's easiest to start the seed off in pots, but if you prefer to sow directly into the soil, you need to start early, to get a long enough growing season. The best way to succeed is by sowing under a clear polythene sheet, but first create a series of troughs and ridges.

- Scoop out trenches 5cm deep with a draw hoe, 30–35cm apart.
- Pile the soil into ridges about 5cm high.

🌱 Sow the seed about 2cm deep into the bottom of the troughs. Stretch the clear polythene over the ridges and secure the edges by burying them. The sweetcorn seedlings will grow in the protected environment under the polythene.

🌱 When the leaves touch the polythene, make a small slit and pull them through to continue growing.

When flowering begins and the grains are swelling, give plants a thorough soak once or twice rather than just wetting the soil surface.

To ensure good pollination, plant groups of at least nine plants at a time as sweetcorn is wind-pollinated. The female flowers (which eventually form the cobs) are pollinated by the male tassels at the top of the plant. You can help by shaking the plants on a still evening when the tassels are fully developed and you'll see clouds of pollen being released. Poor germination will lead to poorly filled, gappy cobs.

TRY THIS
Attacks by mice and slugs can be minimised by raising the seeds in pots and planting out the young plants.

Harvesting and storing

Pick the cobs when the tassels on top have turned brown and shrivelled. Check by peeling back the sheath and press a fingernail into a grain. If the cob is ready, a creamy liquid will squirt out. If the liquid is watery, leave the cob a few days and test it again. Once picked, use as soon as possible.

Stop picking once the grains are doughy when pressed with your nail. This is a sign that the cobs are over-ripe.

SOWING AND GROWING

April	In the mildest areas, sweetcorn can be sown directly in the soil, but it is better to sow in pots to get a head start. Sow one seed per 7cm pot. Use tall pots if possible to avoid disturbing the main root when you plant out later. Germinate the seed somewhere warm. Sweetcorn needs a minimum temperature of 15°C, but the higher the temperature, the faster it will grow.
May	Harden off the plants (see page 63). Delay planting out until all danger of frost has passed. Place the plants 35cm apart to give you one or two cobs per plant. To cut down on weeding later, plant through a sheet mulch. Cover the plants with cloches or garden fleece to protect the young plants from late frosts and cold winds.
June	Plant out in colder areas after the last frost date. Weed between young plants if necessary.
July	On warm, windless days, give plants a gentle nudge to release the pollen from the taller male flowers.
August	In windy areas, use a hoe to heap earth around the stems to stop the plants blowing over as the cobs start to ripen.
October	Pull up the harvested plants and put the remains on the compost heap.

ARTICHOKES

The globe artichoke and the Jerusalem artichoke are two unrelated plants referred to as artichokes. Both offer a rare treat in the kitchen, but also have a place in the ornamental border. Globe artichokes are statuesque focal points with huge blue thistle flowers. Jerusalem artichokes are less spectacular in flower but can be used as a tall temporary hedge for the vegetable plot or as a foliage backdrop in the border instead.

Preparing and caring

Globe artichokes can be grown from seed, though it's easier to buy in small plants.

Mulch established globe artichoke plants with plenty of well-rotted manure or garden compost.

Jerusalem artichokes are not fussy about soil and will tolerate partial shade, though yields will be better in an open position. They are one of the easiest vegetables to grow. Simply plant the tubers about 12cm deep and 30cm apart. They grow up to 1.8m tall and have bright yellow flowers so they make a useful windbreak for the back of the plot. However, in exposed sites, you may need to stake the stems or pile soil around the bases.

GOOD VARIETIES

Globe artichokes
Green Globe
(standard variety)

Purple Globe
(standard variety)

Jerusalem artichoke
'Fuseau' (smooth tubers)

artichokes

5 MINUTE JOB

Cut the dead stems of globe artichokes back to the ground in November. Except in the mildest areas, protect the crowns with straw or cloches.

Harvesting and storing

Multiply your stock of globe artichokes by taking offsets (sideshoots with roots) from the most productive plants and use these to replace existing plants after about three seasons. Although you can start more plants from seed, the resulting plants can be variable. It is much easier to take cuttings from the strongest plants.

Cut off the flower heads of globe artichokes with a little stalk when the outer scales have opened flat as they are now ready to be eaten.

The tubers of Jerusalem artichokes look like small, knobbly potatoes and can be dug up in late autumn and early winter as needed. They should survive light frosts, but in colder areas, cover the crowns with straw. You'll be surprised by how many tubers will be hiding in the soil when you come to dig them up. If you don't want to grow Jerusalem artichokes in the same spot, you'll have to be very thorough, removing any tubers you find or you'll have a forest of plants next summer. Replant one sound, egg-sized tuber for next season.

SOWING AND GROWING

April	**Globe artichokes** Sow in trays in a greenhouse or on a warm windowsill. Transplant the strongest seedlings into individual 7cm pots when large enough. Grow on and gradually harden off the young plants (see page 63). **Jerusalem artichokes** Mail-order suppliers will provide small tubers now. Plant them 10–15cm deep and 30cm apart.
May	**Globe artichokes** Need a sunny but sheltered site and a very rich soil. Allow at least 75cm diameter per plant and dig in plenty of garden compost. **Jerusalem artichokes** Plant out when they are 10cm high. When they reach 1.5–1.8m, pinch out the tops. You will not get the flowers, which look like small sunflowers, but this will encourage tuber formation.
June	Keep newly planted artichokes well watered. **Globe artichokes** On established plants, flower buds should start to appear from June onwards. A well-grown plant should yield up to 12 flowers a year and it will reach up to 1.8m in height.
July	**Globe artichokes** Flowers may form on newly planted globe artichokes, but these are best removed to allow the roots to build up reserves for the following year. **Jerusalem artichokes** When the stems have blackened in the autumn, cut them back to ground level, but mark the position so you can find them easily later for digging up.

THE CABBAGE FAMILY

The principles of growing all large, leafy brassicas are fairly similar. All that really differs is the timing and spacing. All become large plants and take up a fair bit of garden space, but this is usually in the autumn and winter when tender veg has come and gone. They are all slow growing, which means they take up little space when they're young so are ideal for interspersing with quick 'catch crops', such as radishes or salads.

The Cabbage Family

GOOD VARIETIES

'Capriccio' (a Savoy cabbage)

'Hispi' (reliable early pointed variety)

'Minicole' (small round autumn cabbage)

'Primero' (small red cabbage)

'Tundra' (reliable winter cabbage**)**

'Pixie' (spring cabbage)

CABBAGES

Cabbage may not be your first choice for a patio container or an ornamental border, but it can offer the gardener variety and colour in a number of attractive plants all-year round. For example, consider red cabbages with their mauve-tinged outer leaves and tight red hearts, or one of the many hardy winter cabbages, such as 'Tundra'. Both types tend to grow quite large, much wider than the edible hearts themselves.

If lack of space is a problem, consider spring cabbage. They take up little room, keep the ground occupied over winter and will produce a flush of tasty greens in the spring. They will also grow well in an otherwise unoccupied container.

Winter cabbages are some of the largest and most ornamental of the cabbage family. They require plenty of space and a rich soil, but are also a useful source of fresh winter greens. Grow them like summer cabbages, though they do not need to be sown until later in the spring (see page 156). Some types are hardy enough to stand outside over winter, until you need them, while others can be cut in the autumn and stored indoors.

Spring cabbage (spring greens) span the gap from March to May, between the last of the hardy winter varieties and the first of the summer cabbages.

You can also grow and crop modern non-hearting cabbages for most of the year, as a space-saving alternative to the hearting summer and winter varieties. Spring cabbage grows well in containers and can be picked over throughout the winter if they are grown under cover.

Preparing and caring

Cabbages are greedy feeders and will be disappointing on poor soil. They will grow well on heavy clay soil, provided it is not waterlogged, and especially if the soil has had plenty of well-rotted manure dug in over the years.

They also prefer a slightly alkaline soil. If yours is acid (see page 27) you will need to apply garden lime over winter to gradually raise the pH.

On light, sandy soils, an annual application of well-rotted manure or garden compost will help to increase fertility and retain soil moisture. Work up to 170g per sq m of growmore or a similar balanced fertiliser into the soil before sowing or planting out. Four to eight weeks from planting out, scatter a little nitrogenous fertiliser beside the plants and water it in if it does not rain. Reduce the amount of fertiliser to about half if the soil is already well manured.

If you want to start the plants in a seedbed, prepare a small patch of ground, by forking it deeply and raking it down to a fine, level surface. Make seed drills 15cm apart and 2cm deep. Sow the seed thinly, aiming for one every 5cm or so. If the soil is dry, dribble water into the drills before sowing. Cover over with soil and keep the seedbed well watered. Watch out for slugs and flea beetles.

HEALTH WATCH!

Cabbages and their relatives (broccoli, Brussels sprouts, calabrese, cauliflower, kale and oriental greens) can suffer from a large number of pests and diseases. For more details, see pages 153–7.

cabbages

The Cabbage Family

Harvesting and storing

Cut the heads once they have reached full size and feel solid.
Remove any outer leaves, and peel off damaged heart leaves to leave
an unblemished ball.

With spring cabbages, however, you can start by cutting immature
plants as spring greens. You can also pick individual leaves of larger
plants, or leave some to produce firm heads and cut them whole.

TRY THIS
When you harvest spring
cabbages, cut them
off and make a cross-
shaped cut in the top of
the remaining stem. This
will encourage a second
crop of mini cabbages
to form.

Store winter cabbages on racks or trays, not touching, or suspended
in net bags in a cool, dry, airy but frost-free shed or outbuilding. They
should store for up to four months.

Most cabbages can be left in the garden until you need them, but do
not leave them if severe frosts are forecast.

Good to know

Although the cabbage family are attractive to many pests and prone to diseases, most can be prevented by non-chemical methods and good planning.

Cabbage root fly grubs live in the soil and feed on the roots of young plants. Severe attacks can stunt or even kill the plants. To prevent adult flies laying their eggs:

- Push young plants through cabbage collars – 15cm-diameter circles of flexible material, such as carpet underlay, which lie flat on the soil.
- Cover the bed with garden fleece or fine netting supported on plastic hoops. Ensure the edges are well secured. It will also stop other flying pests such as the flea beetle, mealy cabbage aphids and cabbage white butterflies.

Cabbage white butterflies leave their eggs on the plants, which then turn into caterpillars and feed voraciously on the leaves of all members of the cabbage family from mid-summer onwards.

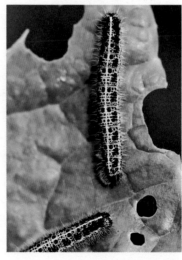

- Check leaves regularly before infestations of caterpillars have a chance to build up. Rub off the tiny eggs or pick off the caterpillars (for the bird table).
- Caterpillars can be killed by spraying with a contact insecticide. One based on pyrethrum is acceptable in organic gardens.
- Fine mesh covers will prevent the female moths laying eggs as long as it is held clear of the leaves.

Flea beetles pepper leaves with little holes (see page 101).

The Cabbage Family

Mealy cabbage aphid can build up rapidly on the undersides of leaves or in the hearts of all brassicas from July onwards and especially in hot summers. The aphids are grey and covered in a waxy excretion, which makes them hard to spray with insecticides. Severe infestations will weaken plants and may also spread virus diseases. Unchecked, they can ruin sprouts and the hearts of cabbages.

🌱 Spray plants thoroughly with a contact insecticide based on soft soap, especially the undersides of leaves.

Pigeons and rabbits relish the leaves of overwintered brassicas.

🌱 Protect the plants by surrounding the plot with rabbit-proof netting, at least 1m tall and buried to a depth of 30cm.

🌱 If pigeons are a problem, cover the crop with netting or humming lines. Make sure netting does not touch the plants, or pigeons will eat the tops.

Whitefly will attack all members of the cabbage family, but are a particular problem on overwintered crops such as sprouting broccoli, where they can survive the winter to infest brassica crops the following spring. Treat as for aphids (see page 41).

SOWING AND GROWING SUMMER AND AUTUMN CABBAGES

February	For the earliest crop, sow a quick-maturing variety in pots. The seed is easy to handle and the germination rate is high. Aim to sow one seed per 7cm pot or one seed per compartment of a 24-module seed tray. Keep them in an unheated greenhouse or other sheltered but frost-free spot, and water regularly.
March	Make the main sowing this month. Choose between a single sowing of an early, a mid-season and a late variety to provide a succession of crops, or monthly sowings of an early variety.
April–May	Plants raised in pots or seedbeds earlier can be planted out now. They should be about 12cm tall, with at least four leaves. Water the pots or seedbed well and handle bare-rooted transplants from seedbeds carefully. Plant so that the base of the first pair of leaves sits on the soil surface, then firm and water in. Allow 45cm diameter per plant in a vegetable plot or border or one plant to a 20cm pot. Space smaller varieties 30cm apart. Cover newly planted cabbages to prevent pests (see page 153–7). Make a further sowing of an early variety, if you have opted for this method of extending the season.
June–July	Harvest early varieties as soon as they produce firm heads. Cabbages in the open are now vulnerable to mealy aphid and caterpillars
August	Mid-season varieties and late-sown early varieties should start to mature.
September–November	Late or autumn cabbage varieties should start to come into their own.

The Cabbage Family

Clubroot is caused by a fungus that can survive in the soil for up to 20 years. Despite feeding and watering, leaves of infected plants will turn red or purple and the plants will wilt on hot days.

- Dig up the plant and you will find the characteristic swollen and distorted roots.
- While a three- or four-year crop rotation may help to prevent a build-up of the disease, once it appears in your garden this will not help to eradicate it. If the disease is restricted to one area, try growing members of the cabbage family on a different part of the garden. Be careful not to transfer soil around the garden, even on your boots. Destroy all affected plants, preferably by burning. Do not compost them.
- Clubroot is less severe in alkaline soil, so liming during the winter to raise the pH to 7.5 will help. Some gardeners take cabbage family plants out of the crop rotation and grow them on the same area year after year. By keeping the plot alkaline through regular liming, they manage to live with clubroot.
- Raise all plants in pots and plant once they are sufficiently well developed so the roots are able to cope with the fungus, so you will still get a crop. Watch out for signs of the disease in ornamental borders; it will also affect related flowers, such as wallflowers, growing there.

SOWING AND GROWING WINTER CABBAGES

May	Sow winter cabbages, either in small pots or in a seedbed as for summer and autumn cabbages.
June	Plant out the young plants into their final position. It is worth planting a quick catch crop to occupy the space around them until they reach full size. Lettuce or radishes are all suitable. Pests are likely to be a nuisance, so cover plants straight away with garden fleece or fine netting, if possible.
July–October	Water in dry spells.
November	Harvest Dutch white cabbages for storing indoors. Other winter cabbages will stand outside until required. Protect overwintered plants from pigeons and rabbits.

Spring cabbage does most of its growing in autumn and winter, so may avoid the disease. There are resistant varieties of most brassica types.

Leaf diseases that can attack the leaves of brassicas include:

- Downy mildew (see page 89).
- Powdery mildew (see page 113).
- Ring spot may occur in cool, wet summers, showing as large spots of concentric rings on older leaves. Destroy badly affected leaves.

Some varieties have resistance to one or more of these diseases. Crop rotation should help to reduce the risk, too. Clear away crop debris at the end of the season and do not compost diseased material.

SOWING AND GROWING SPRING CABBAGES

July	If you live in the north of the UK, this is the best time to sow. Do not forget to water the bottom of the drill thoroughly before you sow at this time of year. Sow in early evening, so that the seeds germinate quickly in moist soil. Cover with fine mesh netting to keep cabbage whites off the young plants – it may become too warm under garden fleece.
August	Sow as for summer and autumn cabbages by the middle of the month if you live in the south.
September	Plant out in the north of the country and colder areas. Space rows 30cm apart and plants every 15cm. This allows for three out of four plants to be picked as greens and the fourth left to heart up. In containers: plant four plants to a 30cm diameter pot.
October	Plant out in southern and milder areas.
November– February	The plants should be large enough to survive the winter. In particularly cold areas, covering with cloches will help to give an earlier crop. Apply a light dressing of a high-nitrogen fertiliser, such as nitrochalk or dried blood, as the plants start into growth.
March–May	Start cutting alternate plants for spring greens as soon as they are large enough. Given enough space, most varieties will produce firm hearts by late April or May.

GOOD VARIETIES

'Clapton' (autumn, clubroot resistant)

'Graffiti' (purple heads)

'Mayflower' (early)

CAULIFLOWERS

Cauliflower is not the easiest vegetable to grow well and it can tie up a lot of space in your garden for quite a time. However, if you want a challenge, it is a crop that can be enjoyed over a long period and by choosing your varieties carefully, you can grow them year-round too. A modern approach is to grow closely spaced baby cauliflowers. As well as producing individual portion-sized curds, it will also leave you room for other crops.

Summer types are sown from early spring for a crop in mid- to late summer. They can also be sown in succession through the summer for cropping into the autumn. These are the best types for baby cauliflowers. You can also sow them in the autumn and overwinter them under cover for an early crop the following spring. **Autumn types** are sown in mid- to late spring for a crop in autumn, usually into November. **Winter types** are also sown in late spring. They are winter-hardy but take longer to mature, producing a head in March to May the following spring.

Preparing and caring

Cauliflowers will do well on heavy clay soil, provided it is not waterlogged. On light soil, dig in lots of well-rotted organic matter. Lime acid soil over winter to give a pH of 7.0 (see page 27). Cauliflowers will also benefit from a generous amount of balanced fertiliser, such as growmore, chicken manure or blood, fish and bone. Work this into the soil before planting out.

Before sowing, decide when you want to harvest the cauliflowers and pick an appropriate variety.

To grow baby cauliflowers plant them closer together. A spacing of 15cm between plants should produce curds about 7.5cm across.

Water young plants in well. Once they are established, do not water unless the soil becomes very dry, as this will encourage lush leaves rather than curds. However, once they are more mature, cauliflowers may bolt or produce undersized curds if the soil gets too dry. A good soak once a week will be more effective than more frequent light watering. Failing that, one really good watering about three weeks before you expect to harvest will boost the size of the head.

TIP
It is easiest to start cauliflowers in pots. But if you sow directly into the ground, take care not to disturb the roots when transplanting – any check to growth can cause them to produce under-sized heads.

Cauliflowers bolt readily. To prevent this, feed and water the seedlings well, transplant them no later than six weeks old, and water in well if it is dry.

⟜ The Cabbage Family

5 MINUTE JOB

Cover cauliflowers straight away with fleece or fine mesh to keep the main pests out, particularly flea beetle, which damages the young plants, and caterpillars that can burrow right into the flower heads.

Prevent insect pests, including caterpillars, which can spoil otherwise perfect curds, by covering the crop with fine mesh. Provided plants are kept well watered and are lifted with the roots as intact as possible, they should not suffer a check.

Harvesting and storing

Check the plants weekly, carefully peeling back the inner leaves. Cut them as soon as the heads reach a decent size. The curds should be white and individual flower buds indistinguishable.

HEALTH WATCH!

See pages 153–7 for details of the many pests and diseases that can affect cabbages and their relatives.

Occasionally, small leaves grow out of the curd. This is caused by fluctuating temperatures and they are still perfectly edible.

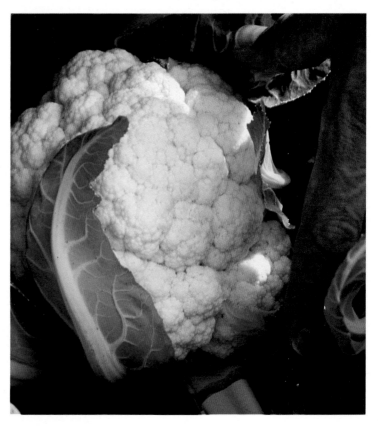

If cabbage whites have been active and you have not taken any control measures, break the curds into pieces and check for caterpillars. Soak the curds in warm, salty water to flush out any hidden caterpillars.

SOWING AND GROWING

February–March	**Summer/autumn types** Ideally, sow in 7cm pots. Keep pots or trays in an unheated greenhouse, coldframe or sheltered spot outside.
April–May	**Summer/autumn types** Plant out cauliflowers raised in pots. For conventional-sized curds, space the plants 45–50cm apart each way. Further sowings of summer varieties will crop from August to early October. **Autumn types** Sow now for harvesting in autumn. Start plants in pots, and plant out after a month or so. **Winter types** Start off hardy winter cauliflowers for a spring crop.
June–July	**All types** If the plants are in the open garden, look out for insect pests (see pages 153–7). **Summer/autumn types** Curds should be ready from the earliest sowings. **Autumn types** These should be growing strongly, but may still benefit from a scattering of high-nitrogen fertiliser along the rows. **Winter types** Plant out winter varieties, 60cm apart each way. Grow a catch crop between them (see page 52).
September–October	**Summer/autumn types** Sow now for an early crop next year. Sow in 7cm pots and keep in an unheated greenhouse or frost-free coldframe over winter. Overwintered plants should be ready to plant out as soon as the soil is in good condition in March and should be a couple of weeks ahead of the earliest spring sowings. Use cloches in colder areas. **Winter types** Boost hardy winter varieties with a dusting of a high-nitrogen fertiliser. The curds should start to form from March to May. To protect them from frost, tie the inner leaves together or break off a couple of the innermost leaves and lay them on top of the developing curd. **Spring types** Plant out every 15cm and in rows 30cm apart.
November–January	**Spring types** The plants should be large enough to survive the winter, but covering with cloches will help to give an earlier crop.
February	**Spring types** Apply a light dressing of a high-nitrogen fertiliser.

GOOD VARIETIES

'Bosworth' (sweeter sprouts)

'Brigitte' (for Christmas)

'Maximus' (for Christmas)

'Petit Posy' (cross between sprouts and kale)

BRUSSELS SPROUTS

It is possible to have fresh Brussels sprouts from August until the spring, but it is as a winter vegetable that they come into their own. Brussels sprouts require rich soil and a lot of space. Since only a small part of the plant is eaten – just the lateral buds formed on the thick single stem – you need a vegetable plot for a reasonable yield. However, even in a small garden, a couple of plants can provide a useful crop for Christmas dinner.

Preparing and caring

Like all brassicas, sprouts prefer a neutral or slightly alkaline soil, which makes them less prone to clubroot (see pages 156–7). Do a simple pH test early on, because if you need to apply lime, this needs to be done at least a month before adding organic matter (see page 27). Dig over the ground where the sprouts will eventually be planted. Add plenty of garden compost or other well-rotted organic matter. The plants will be in the ground a long time so they will need feeding. Fork or rake in 100g a sq m of growmore. Tread down soil before planting. – a firm soil means they are less likely to topple over and the sprouts remain firm for longer.

Keep the ground around the plants weed-free and pick off any caterpillars from the foliage. A month after planting (around June/July), sprinkle a fertiliser such as nitrochalk on the soil surface at 35g a sq m. This adds nitrogen without lowering the pH. Water in if the weather is dry. This is also the time to draw soil around the base of late varieties or to stake plants in an exposed garden. Apply a second dose of nitrochalk in July and water in if the soil is dry.

Use a hoe to keep the weeds down and put up netting if sparrows (or pigeons later in the year) are a problem.

Saving space One plant per 90cm each way is the traditional spacing. You can plant modern varieties closer, at 50–60cm apart each way, but yield drops if you plant any closer, and you increase the risk of fungal diseases. If you are prepared to pick over a shorter period, try an early variety at 50cm apart each way.

Alternatively, use the space between young plants for another crop. Lettuce, radish, summer spinach, beetroot and early carrot will be ready before the sprouts need the space.

To avoid picking your sprouts off the ground when you come to harvest, stake plants with sturdy canes.

Remove any dead or dying leaves around the bottom of plants every week or so. This helps remove a source of disease, allows air to circulate and makes picking the sprouts easier.

5 MINUTE JOB

To encourage your Brussels sprouts plants to develop properly, cut off the top of the stem. The individual sprouts will then swell and you can eat the removed top as if it were cabbage.

The Cabbage Family

Harvesting and storing

Harvesting time is not critical with sprouts; they will stay on the plant until you are ready to pick them and most can be picked over a three- month period. Some varieties are particularly noted for their 'standing time', a characteristic worth looking out for if you want to pick little and often over the winter.

Harvest when the sprouts are tightly closed buttons. Starting at the bottom of the stalk, either pull them off with your fingers or cut them off with a sharp knife. While you are harvesting, you can also remove and destroy any yellowing foliage or open sprouts.

Picking sprouts after they have thawed from a frost is said to make them taste sweeter, but you can pick them before if you want to. In cold weather, uproot whole plants and leave them outside the kitchen door. The sprouts can then be picked off indoors when they are needed. Picked sprouts will keep for a couple of days in the salad compartment of a fridge, but if you have a lot, it is worth freezing them.

SOWING AND GROWING

March	Sow seed from mid-March to mid-April. For just a few plants, sow seed in 9cm pots. You do not need a greenhouse; the pots can be kept outside in a sheltered spot or in a coldframe. You need to keep an eye on them to make sure the compost is moist but not sodden or dry. For more than a dozen plants, use the seedbed technique to start them off (see page 53). Sow seed 1.5cm deep in rows 15cm apart. Seed will germinate in one to two weeks. Thin the seedlings to 8cm apart or one per pot.
April	There is still time to sow seed for a winter crop so long as you do it before the middle of the month. Prepare soil for planting if not yet done and leave the ground to settle.
May	Early sowings should be ready for planting out by early May; later sowings by mid-May to early June. When the seedlings are 15cm high they are ready to be moved on to their final planting site. Water the rows the day before and ease up the young plants with a trowel, taking care not to damage or dry out the roots. Dig a hole with the trowel and plant so the lower leaves are just above the soil surface. Firm down well and water them in well. Allow 50–90cm between the plants.
June	Aim to complete planting by the beginning of this month.
October–January	If you prefer to harvest and freeze sprouts in one go, cut off the leafy head at the top of the plant. This will encourage the sprouts to mature all at once. However, there is no reason to do this if you want to pick little and often. The leafy tops can be left and used as spring greens.

GOOD VARIETIES

'Brokali Apollo' (quick tenderstem type)

'Green Magic'

'Ironman'

'Marathon' (reliable older variety)

CALABRESE

Although it originated in Italy, calabrese or green broccoli – to distinguish it from white and purple sprouting broccoli (see pages 169–71) – is sometimes known, confusingly, as American broccoli or plain broccoli in the supermarkets.

By careful choice of variety and planting dates it is possible to have fresh calabrese from the garden for much of the year. You have the choice of growing close together and harvesting just the main heads, or further apart for a crop of side shoots too.

Calabrese will suffer a setback to its growth if it is transplanted from a seedbed, producing a poor-sized head. It is therefore best to start it off in pots, so that it can be planted out without disturbing the rootball.

Preparing and caring

Calabrese grows best in a rich soil. If possible, dig in well-rotted manure or garden compost before planting. If this is impractical, work in a balanced fertiliser instead. A light dressing of a nitrogen fertiliser can be given when the young plants have 6–8 leaves, to boost yields.

HEALTH WATCH!

Calabrese suffers from the whole range of cabbage family pests and diseases (see pages 153–7).

Improve the yield of calabrese by giving the plants a good soaking about a month or so after planting out, especially if the summer is dry.

Bear in mind that cabbage white caterpillars start to become troublesome during mid-summer and will severely damage young plants given the chance, so cover the plants with fine netting.

The Cabbage Family

Harvesting and storing

The flower buds that make up the head should be tight and completely green. Yellow flowers will start to show if the heads are left too long before cutting.

Cut the heads with as much stalk as possible. This and any leaves can be trimmed off before cooking. At this stage, you can remove the plants and replace them with another crop, or leave them to develop several flushes of smaller side shoots.

SOWING AND GROWING

February– March	Make the first sowing in pots in a greenhouse or somewhere you can maintain a temperature of at least 13°C. Sow two seeds to a 7cm pot. If both germinate, pull out the weaker one later. Keep the plants growing somewhere frost-free. The compost needs to be moist but try to avoid wetting the leaves, as they are very susceptible to downy mildew.
April–May	Plant out the first sowing after six to eight weeks. In cold areas, plant them under cloches or garden fleece. Space plants 15cm apart in rows 30cm apart. For a follow-on crop of side shoots, space them 30cm apart each way. Water plants while in their pots and try not to disturb the rootball when planting out. Plant them deeply, so the first set of leaves are level with the soil surface. Sow further small batches throughout April and May for a long harvest. As the weather warms up, you can start plants off in pots in a sheltered spot outdoors or sow seed directly where they are to grow.
June–July	Continue to sow small batches of seed and plant out earlier sowings, protecting them at all times from cabbage whites. Cut the main heads of earlier sowings and pick over the side shoots of the earliest batch before the flower buds start to open.
August	Make a last sowing for a crop before Christmas. Note that the plants will be killed by severe frost.
September	Plant out the late-sown plants and continue to pick over early crops.
October	Cover late crops planted out last month with tall cloches or garden fleece. Continue to cut main heads and side shoots of later sowings.

SPROUTING BROCCOLI

Broccoli is often used as a catch-all term for a number of vegetables, ranging from coloured types of cauliflower to calabrese. But true or sprouting broccoli produces lots of smaller buds at the ends of side shoots rather than fewer, larger heads. Sprouting broccoli is more of a 'cut-and-come-again' vegetable, so you can pick small amounts of it over a period of several weeks or months.

Sprouting broccoli comes into its own in the winter and early spring, when fresh vegetables are most welcome. It needs a fair amount of space over a long growing season, so it is only really worth growing if you have a vegetable plot. However, it does occupy ground in late winter and early spring that would otherwise be unproductive.

GOOD VARIETIES

'Claret'

'Red Arrow'

'Rioja'

sprouting broccoli

Preparing and caring

Prepare a seedbed by digging over the soil and rake the surface to a fine texture before making a drill about 1.5cm deep. Water the bottom of the drill if the soil is dry. Unless it is exceptionally cold, cloches are not necessary, though you may need to take precautions against slugs and flea beetles.

The only major pest is likely to be pigeons as long as the plants are big and healthy when they go into the winter (although see also 'Health watch!', left). Cover plants with pigeon netting if this is a problem.

Broccoli requires a fairly rich soil with plenty of nitrogen. Depending on the previous crop, apply a top-dressing of a nitrogen fertiliser, such as nitrochalk or dried blood. Water this in if it does not rain the next day.

Harvesting and storing

Pick the flower shoots as they develop between January and May. The purple or white flower buds should still be tight with no sign of the yellow flowers.

Leave the small tender leaves around the flower buds and the flower stalk, all of which are edible. Spears may develop over a long period from just after (sometimes before) Christmas until well into May. Keep picking regularly to prevent the plants flowering.

SOWING AND GROWING

April–May	Make a single sowing of sprouting broccoli. Bear in mind that the plants need plenty of space, so do not sow too many. Sow two seeds per 7cm pot. Broccoli is a hardy plant and will germinate at low temperatures, provided it does not fall below freezing. If both seeds germinate, pull out the weaker one. Alternatively, sow the seed thinly into drills 1.5cm deep and 10cm apart. Aim for a seed every 10cm or so.
June–July	Transplant the young plants into their final position. Water the seedbed or pots well first and try to retain as many roots as possible on bare-rooted transplants. Space plants 60cm apart each way. Until the plants reach full size you can grow a catch crop in the spaces between them, such as lettuce and spinach (see page 52).
August	Keep an eye out for cabbage white caterpillars on the leaves (see page 153).
September–October	The plants should be large and leafy as they go into the winter. In exposed gardens, earth up the base of the plants or stake them to stop them blowing over.

The Cabbage Family

GOOD VARIETIES

'Black Tuscany' (long puckered leaves)

'Scarlet' (frilly purple leaves)

'Starbor' (frilly green leaves)

TIP
If the leaves start to change colour, the plants may be running out of nutrients. Either feed them with a liquid feed, or pot on into a larger pot.

HEALTH WATCH!

Flea beetles, aphids and cabbage white butterflies can be problems (see pages 153–7).

Slugs may also damage the young plants (see pages 40–1) and, later in the season, keep an eye out for **mealy cabbage aphid** (see page 154), which can build up very rapidly, unnoticed.

KALE
Once confined to the allotment as a standby for the 'hungry gap' period of late winter and early spring, kale is now appreciated for its appearance, too. Modern and rediscovered heritage varieties are worth adding to ornamental borders and containers, especially as winter fillers.

Kale can be grown as a cut-and-come-again salad crop (see page 94) and if left to bolt in the spring, the immature flower shoots rival sprouting broccoli.

Preparing and caring

Traditionally, kale is started off in a seedbed. Draw a shallow (1.5–2cm deep) drill in well-prepared soil (see page 53 for more details). Water the bottom well.

Cover seedbeds with garden fleece to prevent attacks from pests and use bird netting or bird scarers over winter if pigeons are a problem in your garden or up at the allotment.

The Cabbage Family

Harvesting and storing

Pick individual younger leaves as required. Wash them carefully to remove any aphids or whitefly lurking in the wrinkles.

The immature flower shoots (before the yellow flowers start to show) can be picked and eaten like sprouting broccoli. You should also get a flush of tender young leaves before the plants bolt.

SOWING AND GROWING

April–May	Sow seed thinly across the seedbed, aiming for one every 5cm or so. Cover with soil. If you want only a few plants for a container or border, start the seed off in 7cm pots. The seed is quite large and easy to handle – sow two per pot and pull out the weaker one if both germinate. A cool but frost-free place in the garden or an unheated room is fine, with a minimum temperature of 5°C.
June	Grow the young plants in pots on in a sheltered spot outdoors.
July	Plant out into their final position. Water the pot or the seedbed well. Make a slight depression and plant into the bottom. This allows easier watering in a dry summer, until the plants are established. Lift the young plants carefully from the seedbed with as much root as possible. They may flop after planting even if well watered, but will quickly recover. For larger varieties, space the plants 45cm apart each way. For containers: use a pot that holds at least 5 litres of compost and site it where you can water it frequently. Smaller varieties can be grown as baby vegetables planted as close as 15cm apart.
August–October	Consider a crop of kale as a gap-filler in August, after early crops have been harvested. Sow the seed directly into drills and thin out in stages to leave the final spacing. You can use thinnings in salad. Slugs and flea beetles should not cause further problems on established plants.
March–April	The plants might start to look scruffy and the leaves unappetising, but leave them to bolt for the edible flower shoots.

SWEDES, TURNIPS AND KOHL RABI

You may think winter turnips and swedes only have a place in the traditional allotment. But many smaller turnip varieties take as little as eight weeks from sowing to eating, so they make excellent catch crops. Kohl rabi is a continental relative of the turnip and is a decorative substitute worth considering in even the smallest garden.

The larger varieties of turnips and all the swedes (originally an abbreviation for Swedish turnip, after their origin) are slow growing and produce large roots that can be stored for winter use. The smaller, summer turnips and kohl rabi, which produce an edible swollen stem above ground, rather than a root, are grown as summer crops.

GOOD VARIETIES

Swede
'Marian' (reliable older variety)

Turnips
'Armand' (purple topped)

'Golden Ball' (golden winter turnip)

Summer turnips
'Sweet Bell'

'Snowball'

Kohl rabi
'Logo'

The Cabbage Family

HEALTH WATCH!

Although swede, turnip and kohl rabi can be attacked by all the usual cabbage family pests – **flea beetle, cabbage aphid, whitefly and cabbage caterpillars** – because it's the root you eat, the most troublesome is the **cabbage root fly** (see pages 153–7).

Kohl rabi is less severely affected by **cabbage root fly** than turnips and swedes. Some varieties of swede have an in-built resistance to **clubroot**. Liming the soil will also help prevent damage.

Preparing and caring

Summer turnips and kohl rabi need a moist, fertile soil, but will tolerate light shade during the summer. They also do best on a slightly alkaline soil. Because it forms globes above rather than below ground, kohl rabi is better able to cope with heavy soil than turnips. Prepare the soil by forking and raking to create a seedbed. Work in a reasonable amount of balanced fertiliser and water the soil a couple of days before sowing if it is dry.

In dry spells, water regularly – give a generous soak once a week to wet the soil thoroughly.

Maincrop varieties of turnip are much slower growing, and swedes are slow growers. Both are left to mature for storing through the winter. They are not particularly fussy but, like all members of the cabbage family, do best in a slightly alkaline soil. If necessary, apply lime during the previous winter. They do not need organic matter but, ideally, should follow a crop manured the previous year. If not, they will need a balanced fertiliser. Grow them in the same crop-rotation group as other cabbage family members.

The Cabbage Family

Summer turnips and kohl rabi are useful catch crops. Because they are related to the larger members of the cabbage family, they are usually grown in the same crop-rotation group.

- Use them to fill space from February to June before winter crops such as sprouting broccoli or winter cauliflowers are planted out.
- Sow them in May between Brussels sprout plants. These will not need all their allotted space until later in the summer, by which time the catch crop is ready to be harvested.
- Grow them after an early crop of broad beans or early peas have been cleared, so they benefit from the nitrogen left by the previous crop.

SOWING AND GROWING SUMMER TURNIPS AND KOHL RABI

February	An early sowing of turnips can be made under cloches. In colder areas or for growing outside, wait until March.
March	It should be safe to sow turnips directly outside, but leave kohl rabi until the end of the month. Both crops can be grown close together to produce lots of small baby roots. They can be sown little and often through the summer. Make seed drills 1.5cm deep and 15cm apart. Sow the seed thinly, to avoid having to thin out later. Both crops can be used as a catch crop (see above) and will succeed in containers. Scatter the seed thinly and cover with about 1.5cm of compost. Thin the seedlings to roughly 7.5–10cm apart. In a border: sow small patches of kohl rabi and thin out later, or start the seed off in pots.
April	Sow another batch and thin out the earlier sowings to give roughly one plant every 10cm for larger roots, or 3cm for baby roots. You do not need to be too thorough, as the roots will push apart as they grow.
May–July	For tender roots, the plants should grow rapidly without any check to their growth. The first roots should be ready in early May. Start to pull them as soon as they reach golf-ball size. Sow further batches at fortnightly intervals if you want to extend the harvest into autumn.
August–September	Continue to pull the later sowings as soon as they reach either golf-ball or just before tennis-ball size.

Harvesting and storing

Both turnips and kohl rabi are best harvested before they reach tennis-ball size. Trim off the long root and outer leaves of kohl rabi, leaving the swollen stem with just a small tuft of immature leaves. Both can be eaten raw; young turnips are an alternative to radish.

Start to lift the roots of winter turnips and swedes as soon as they are large enough – you do not have to wait until they reach full size. Keep them in a cool but frost-free place until required. Swede is generally regarded as sweeter and milder in flavour than turnip.

SOWING AND GROWING WINTER TURNIPS AND SWEDES

May–June	Make a single sowing of swede for winter use. Make seed drills 2cm deep and 35–40cm apart. Sow very thinly to avoid having to thin out later. Both crops can be started in pots or modules. If space in the vegetable plot will not be available until late July, this is a good option. It also saves thinning.
July–August	Maincrop turnips are usually sown later. Space the rows 30cm apart. Thin both crops early to avoid damaging the roots. If necessary, thin out in stages to leave 15cm between turnips and 23cm between swedes. They do not need regular watering, but make sure the soil does not dry out completely or they will become tough and woody.
September–October	Both crops should be ready for lifting with a fork. They can be left in situ until the New Year, or lifted and stored.

THE ONION FAMILY

Onions aren't expensive to buy in the shops, but all the same, it is relatively easy to be self-sufficient in them for most of the year. Work out how many you need from late summer to the following spring and simply plant that number. Shallots have a sweeter taste and cost more to start with, but they store for ages. And as for leeks and garlic: well, these are two of the easiest crops to grow.

GOOD VARIETIES

Onions
'Centurion' (brown onion set)

'Forum' (brown onion set)

'Red Baron' (reliable red from sets)

'Troy' (autumn planted sets)

'Vision' (good from seed)

Shallots
'Golden Gourmet' (round yellow)

'Longor' (long French shallot)

'Mikor' (round, pink tinged)

ONIONS AND SHALLOTS

Onions must be one of the easiest vegetables to grow, especially if you start from sets. Each small set will grow into a full-sized onion during the summer. On a vegetable plot, onion plants need very little attention and can be left to mature and dry off for winter storage. It should be possible to store homegrown onions until the following spring. Onions will grow and produce a worthwhile crop in large containers, too. There is now a good choice of varieties from sets.

With more flavour and less pungency than onions, shallots are also a versatile ingredient in the kitchen, delicious roasted or in casseroles. As they are expensive in the supermarket, they must be worth the space in any garden.

Preparing and caring

When you buy onion sets, you are buying immature onions that were raised from seed the previous summer. Because they are sown at a very high density, they do not reach sufficient size to bolt or produce flowers in the second season – they just carry on growing instead. Under normal conditions, onions are biennial, producing a bulb in the first year and flowering the second season. Sets are a convenient way of cutting out the seedling stage. Some varieties are more prone to bolting in their second year, but are usually heat-treated to prevent this.

Prepare the ground by digging the soil to loosen it. Soil that is too compact or firm will cause the onion roots to push the sets out as they grow. The ideal site is a piece of well-cultivated, weed-free ground that has been manured in previous years but not recently. Onions benefit from a little balanced fertiliser (up to 35g a sq m of growmore or similar), but do not add fresh manure before planting.

Shallots have a sweeter taste and cost more to start with, but store for ages. Shallots are an unfussy vegetable. They will do well on any reasonably well-drained, fertile soil and prefer a neutral pH. They need only a little general fertiliser and in most years will not need to be watered. Use a trowel to avoid damaging them as you bury them – about 15cm apart in rows 30cm apart, or 23cm apart each way in raised beds.

HEALTH WATCH!

Downy mildew affects the leaves (see page 89). If bulbs are affected, they become soft and will not store. Destroy all affected plants and don't replant onions or shallots on that spot for five years. There are no chemical controls available. Look for resistant varieties.

White rot is the most serious disease of onions. It is very persistent and remains in the soil for up to 18 years. The leaves turn yellow prematurely and wilt. A white, fluffy mould with minute black spots grows on the bulbs. It spreads rapidly, so destroy all infected plants. The only solution is to grow onions and related crops on a new site in subsequent years. Take care not to spread soil from infected areas on footwear and tools. There are no chemical controls.

The Onion Family

Birds will pull out the sets given the chance, so cover them with garden fleece or a cloche.

As the onions and shallots grow, hoe between the rows, and if necessary hand-weed between the plants. You can buy special short-handled onion hoes that allow you to bend or kneel down to hoe. Even when fully grown, onions cannot shade out other plants so they are very sensitive to weed competition. In most years, onions do not need additional watering.

In late summer, the foliage will start to yellow and fall over naturally. Let nature take its course – if you bend them over too early, the leaves can get damaged and let in diseases.

SOWING AND GROWING ONIONS

January	Buy onion sets. Look out for the small bulbs in garden centres. Choose ones that are firm to the touch and store them in a dry place, ready for planting.
February	As soon as the soil is workable and not too wet, you can plant onion sets. In cold areas or on heavy soil, delay until mid-March or even April. Sow onion seed indoors.
March–April	Push the sets gently into the soil so the tips are just buried. The spacing will, to some extent, determine the final size of the bulbs. For lots of small bulbs, about 5cm in diameter, plant the sets 5cm apart in rows 15cm apart. This spacing allows room to get a hoe between the rows. This is important as onions cannot compete with weeds, so you will need to hoe or weed by hand. As the onions grow, the bulbs will push each other apart. For larger bulbs (up to 10cm across), increase the spacing to 10cm within the rows. In containers: push sets into the compost 7.5–10cm apart each way.
August–September	Lift the bulbs with a fork to break the roots and leave them on the surface to ripen fully in the sun. In a wet summer, cover them with cloches or move them to a greenhouse bench to complete their ripening. You can plant autumn onion sets early in September in the north, later in the south.
October	Lift the spring crop for storing.

The Onion Family

TRY THIS

Don't waste spare onion or shallot sets. Plant them close together in pots and snip the young shoots with scissors for an early crop of salad onions.

Harvesting and storing

If some plants have bolted, the bulbs are still edible, but use these as soon as possible as they will not store well.

Store sound onions in a cool, dry, airy place through the winter. If you don't want to plait onions into the traditional strings, you can tie them in tights or store them in net sacks.

You can also spread bulbs in a single layer in shallow trays. Inspect them regularly and immediately throw out any that show signs of mould, rotting or softening.

Fully-ripened shallots should store well into the following winter and early spring. Spread them out in a single layer on wooden trays or wire racks, and then keep them in a cool, dry place. If you keep the shallots beyond New Year, ensure that you check occasionally for signs of rotting.

SOWING AND GROWING SHALLOTS

March	If the soil is still cold and wet, delay planting until April. Prepare the site by forking over to loosen the soil. Work in a little general fertiliser, unless the area has been manured for a previous crop. Do not add organic matter when growing shallots. Push the individual bulbs into the soil so the tips are just covered. Birds may pull them out if they are visible. Give them more space than onion sets, 15cm apart in rows 30cm apart should be fine. You could space them 23cm apart each way in a raised bed, but allow enough space for hoeing between the plants later.
April	Aim to complete planting by early April.
May–June	Keep weeds under control.
July	As soon as the top starts to dry off, lift the clump of bulbs out of the soil to expose it to the sun. Leave the bulbs to dry and ripen in the sun. But cover them with cloches or bring them indoors to complete drying in wet weather.
August	Lift and store bulbs when fully ripe.

LEEKS

Leeks make a very useful winter vegetable. They are so hardy you can leave them in the ground until you need them. Baby leeks are easy to grow in containers and raised vegetable beds and provide a tasty crop through the summer and autumn. Grow some on into conventional-sized leeks for winter. In the border, the strap-shaped, blue-green leaves are an interesting addition throughout the winter.

Leeks are very easy to grow from seed and because you can transplant them without a problem they are very versatile. Start them in pots ready to plant out later in the season to follow other crops that have been harvested. Or grow them in a seedbed, use the thinnings as an alternative to spring onions, and plant them into their final position for a winter crop.

Preparing and caring
Baby leeks have become popular in supermarkets and are the best option for containers and raised beds.

- Sow short rows regularly from March to June in seed drills 15cm apart. Thin the seedlings, if necessary, to about 1cm apart. In containers, sow seed roughly 2.5cm apart and cover with a dusting of compost.
- Keep the young plants well watered so that they grow rapidly and produce tender young plants about as thick as a pencil.
- Pull these in bunches and use them as a substitute for spring onions. They are a little milder and can be used in salads or braised.
- You can also leave them to grow on and pull them as baby leeks when they reach 1–1.5cm in diameter.

GOOD VARIETIES

'Apollo' (reliable late crop)

'Bandit' (reliable late crop)

'Darwin' (reliable late crop)

'Striker' (good as a baby leek)

'Zermatt' (good baby leek)

The Onion Family

Allium leaf miner affects leeks and related crops, and until recently was confined to an area west of Birmingham. White grubs mine the leaves, causing clear patches, and move down into the bulb, overwintering as orange-brown pupae 3–4mm long. Cover your leeks with fleece or fine mesh.

Leek moth is more severe in late summer, especially in hot weather. The yellow-green caterpillars burrow in the leaves and into the base of the leek, allowing rot to enter. Removing damaged leaves may help the plant to recover. Cover your leeks with fleece or fine mesh.

Leek rust results in raised, rust-coloured spots or streaks on the leaves. In severe cases, leaves may turn yellow and die. Remove and burn badly affected plants. The blanched underground stems of mildly affected plants are still edible and the plants will stand through the winter. Destroy the remains of the crop and grow on a new piece of ground each year.

Harvesting and storing

Leeks need no protection from the cold, but bear in mind that lifting leeks from frozen ground is hard work. If very cold spells are forecast, lift a supply of leeks and plant them temporarily in a sheltered part of the garden. Always use a fork pushed deeply beside the plant to ease it out of the ground.

In colder areas cover the seedbeds with cloches or garden fleece once you have sown the seeds. Remove the cloche or fleece covers from seedbeds once the young plants resemble rows of grass.

To plant leeks, drop each plant into a hole made with a dibber – the end of an old spade handle is perfect – or a narrow trowel. The deeper the hole, the longer the blanched stem will be, but make sure that some of the leaves are above soil level.

Fill each hole with water to settle the plants in. They will flop at first but will soon pick up. The holes will fill in, too.

SOWING AND GROWING

March	March is early enough to make the first sowing. The young plants will also be at the right stage to follow on early crops such as early potatoes, early peas or broad beans in late June or July. If you want lots of plants for a vegetable plot, sow in a seedbed. Make seed drills 1–2cm deep and 15cm apart. Sow fairly thickly as the thinnings can be used for salads. Leek seeds will germinate at fairly low temperatures (around 7°C). For borders: start seed off in small pots or modular trays. Sow seed about 2.5cm apart in seed trays. Keep them somewhere cool but frost-free. They can be slow to germinate and reach a good size.
April–May	After careful hardening off (see page 63), move plants raised inside outdoors when temperatures start to rise. Prick out the seedlings into modular trays to grow on. Do not worry if you cannot separate every seedling. Thin seed rows out to leave a plant every 3–4cm.
June	Depending on the growth of the young leeks and when space becomes available, plant out into the final position. The plants will wait until you are ready, but should ideally be about 20cm tall and as thick as a pencil. Plant leeks raised in pots or modules into the bottom of a shallow depression. Use a draw hoe to make a trench about 10cm wide and deep. This will make earthing up, to blanch the base of the plant, easier later.
July	Water plants raised in a seedbed then ease them out of the soil with a fork. Separate them out and trim the roots to 8–10cm. You can trim very long leaves too to compensate. Aim for a plant every 15cm in rows 30cm apart for average-sized leeks. Increasing or decreasing the spacing will produce bigger or smaller leeks.
August–September	Leeks planted with a dibber should have a long white stem. Other plants can be earthed up as they grow, by drawing soil along the row to increase the length of blanched stem.
October–Spring	Harvest the leeks as you need them through the winter (see opposite). After you've finished harvesting the crop, prepare the site for its next crop by forking the soil deeply, especially if it is compacted. At the same time, work in some general fertiliser. Give the whole area a thorough soaking if the soil is dry and leave for a week to settle.

The Onion Family

GOOD VARIETIES

'Apache' (purple)

'Lilia' (purple)

'Green Banner' (white)

'Performer' (white)

'White Lisbon – Winter Hardy' (for winter)

SPRING ONIONS

Salad onions, often called spring onions, are immature onions that are used raw in salads or as a garnish. Their small size also makes them ideal for stir-fries. You can get a worthwhile crop of salad onions from the smallest space, be it a container, small raised bed or border. They are ready to harvest in 10–12 weeks, so you can sow every fortnight in spring for a continuous supply all through the summer. Some extra-hardy varieties will overwinter, which means that you can pull your own salad onions the following spring.

Preparing and caring

Water weekly for tender, succulent salad onions in dry weather to keep the plants growing rapidly.

Harvesting and storing

Pull bunches of plants as soon as the stems are 1cm thick. Some varieties will have a distinct bulb at the base, others will not.

SOWING AND GROWING

February	Make the first sowing under cloches.
March–July	Start to sow outdoors from mid-March. Make several sowings, either in pots of multipurpose compost or in patches in the border. In a vegetable plot or raised bed, sow short rows or bands, once a fortnight for a summer-long supply. In containers: scatter seeds roughly 2–3cm apart, and cover with about 1.5cm of compost. In the garden, sow in rows 10cm apart and thin the seedlings to 2.5cm apart.
August	For an early crop the following spring, sow a hardy winter variety now.

GARLIC

Garlic is one of the easiest crops to grow. No matter where you live in the UK, so long as you have a weed-free, sunny spot and well-drained soil, you can grow garlic just by planting a single clove and waiting until a whole bulb is ready to harvest. Since ancient times, it has been known for its curative properties, and is used in almost every cuisine in the world.

Preparing and caring

Garlic requires little attention while it grows. All you need do is pull up any weeds that come up near the plants. If the weather is very dry, it is worth watering to encourage leaf growth, as this determines the size of the bulb.

Garlic is one of the easiest to be self-sufficient in. If a bulb of garlic lasts you two weeks in the kitchen, plant two bulbs in later winter or early spring. Don't be tempted to plant one that you've bought from a supermarket as the results can be disappointing.

A garlic bulb should break into 10–12 cloves for planting. If the cloves push out of the ground as they grow, simply use a trowel to plant them deeper.

HEALTH WATCH!

Garlic can suffer from the same soil-borne diseases as onions and leeks, especially **leek rust** (see pages 183 and 188). Do not plant garlic where onions and leeks have been growing previously, and start with healthy cloves.

Plant spare cloves in pots of multipurpose compost and harvest the green shoots like chives. If you have a large crop of bulbs, try planting a couple of whole bulbs in a pot, or leave them in the ground. Early the following spring they will produce a clump of green shoots that can be cut and used in the same way as chives.

Harvesting and storing

Loosen the soil with a hand fork and ease the bulbs out gently. Dry them in the sun or on a sunny windowsill in case of summer showers.

Put bulbs in a clean seed tray or plait the leaves and hang them up. Store them somewhere dry at a minimum of 5°C. Garlic stored in this way should keep successfully until the following spring.

SOWING AND GROWING

February	In milder areas, garlic can be planted now, if the soil is workable and not too wet. Loosen heavy or compacted soil.
March	Plant out in colder areas as soon as the soil is in good condition. Separate the bulb into individual cloves and plant each one upright, with the flat base of the clove facing downwards. Push them at least 3cm down into the soil with no tip visible or birds will pull them up. Leave 10–25cm between each clove. The bigger the clove, the larger the space needed.
June–July	Bulbs should start to swell underground. As soon as the leaves turn yellow, harvest the garlic. If left, the bulbs might re-sprout and not store so well.
October–November	Garlic can also be planted in autumn (late October to early November). Push the cloves in firmly so that they are not lifted out by early frost. Otherwise they need no attention and should be ready to harvest the following June or July.

ROOT CROPS

Root vegetables are wonderfully easy to grow. They are cool-weather crops, ready to be harvested in the spring or autumn. Give them well-drained, loose soil and they will grow big and fat ready to be dug up and eaten straightaway or stored to be enjoyed over the coming months. Just make sure you sort out the damaged vegetables or any showing signs of rot and use them first.

GOOD VARIETIES

'Cara' (maincrop)

'Charlotte' (best tasting salad type)

'Lady Christl' (early)

'Sarpo Mira' (blight resistant maincrop)

POTATOES

If you have a vegetable plot, you can grow the whole range of potato types, including maincrops to store through the winter. However, you do not need an allotment to grow potatoes – all you need is a decent-sized container (at least ten litres) to grow a crop of tasty new potatoes in the smallest garden. You can even grow several container crops throughout the year, including, if you so wish, new potatoes for Christmas dinner.

Preparing and caring

Generally, potatoes are an easy crop, though there are some potential problems. Most can be prevented by a few simple precautions.

- Always buy certified seed potatoes. Do not save your own tubers.
- Follow a three- or preferably four-year crop rotation (see pages 21–3).
- Work in plenty of organic matter on dry soil to retain moisture and help prevent the diseases scab and spraing.

🌱 Control aphids, which can spread viruses, as soon as you see them.

🌱 Earth up the plants to help prevent blight (if it occurs) affecting the tubers. To prevent scab, do not lime the soil the previous winter.

Prepare the ground in January if you did not do so before Christmas. Dig the area deeply to loosen it and if you have well-rotted manure available, work this in at the same time. You can leave the surface fairly rough. On light soils it can be worthwhile preparing a trench (see page 34), but this is not essential on most soils. Use a spade or trowel to bury individual tubers about 15cm deep. A potato planter will make the job even easier. Apply a mulch of well-rotted garden compost – this will be incorporated into the soil by worms and also as you earth up the rows.

TIP
If frost is predicted, cover the foliage with garden fleece, cloches, straw or sacking. The foliage is easily blackened or killed by frost and the yield will be reduced.

When the first shoots appear above the soil surface, use a draw hoe or a soil rake to start to draw earth from between the rows over the centre of the row, to cover the shoots. Earthing up encourages underground shoots and hence more tubers. It also prevents tubers pushing above the surface and turning green, and protects young shoots from frost. Keep doing this at intervals until you end up with a flat, round-topped ridge roughly 30cm high and across.

Early potatoes will benefit from a thorough soaking each week in dry weather and when the tubers are swelling during June and July.

Do not water maincrops until later in the summer when the tubers are forming – you will only encourage leaves. Then, in August when flowers start to appear, give them a thorough soaking if the weather is dry and scatter general fertiliser along the row.

To grow potatoes in pots, plant tubers at the bottom of a large tub and just cover them with compost. As the potatoes grow, keep adding more compost until the pots are full. This encourages more tubers to form and stops them being pushed out of the compost later and turning green. Check the weight of the tub and water when it feels light.

Harvesting and storing

Start digging early potatoes as soon as there are decent-sized tubers. Try pushing your hand under a plant and feel for egg-sized tubers. An alternative is to lift a plant gently with a fork. If the tubers are still immature, replant it and give it a good soaking.

With maincrops, if the tubers start to get too big before you need them, cut off the tops and leave them in the ground until you want them. This will also help prevent blight spoiling them. Remove as many tubers as you can, even the smallest. 'Volunteer' potatoes always seem to pop up where you least want them the following year. They can also carry blight.

To avoid spearing tubers with the fork, push it in about 30cm from the dead top and push under the plant. Lift the potatoes on a dry day. Spread them out in a dark shed for a day or two to dry off completely. Sort out any that have been damaged by slugs or the fork and use them immediately.

Store sound, dry tubers in hessian or double paper sacks until spring, when they shrivel and start to sprout.

Good to know

Eelworms are minute worm-like creatures that attack the roots of potatoes. The first signs are weak plants that start to wilt. Reddish-brown cysts the size of a pinhead can be seen on the roots. Eelworm is very persistent. Destroy all traces of the affected crop and do not grow potatoes on that area for eight years.

Slugs can be a major problem on heavy and wet soil (see pages 40–1), although early varieties may be less affected, and early lifting of maincrops may help to reduce damage.

Blackleg is a bacterial disease that causes the leaves to roll and wilt, and the stems to blacken. It usually occurs early in the season and in dry weather. Destroy any affected plants.

Blight is a serious disease of potatoes. It starts as small brown spots or blotches on the leaves from June onwards, especially in warm, wet spells. Plants may die gradually, and neighbouring potatoes and tomatoes can be infected. Spores washing into the soil will affect tubers, which will then rot.

- Earthing up will help prevent this happening.
- A more drastic alternative is to cut off and destroy affected foliage to prevent spores infecting the tubers.
- Blight can be prevented by spraying with a copper-based fungicide, before symptoms first appear. Repeat this treatment every two weeks.

Scab is caused by a fungus and is worse in light and limy soils. Plenty of organic matter and watering during a hot summer will help. Affected tubers can be eaten after peeling.

Spraing is caused by a virus spread by small worms in the soil. The tubers appear normal until cut open, when brown marks are seen in the flesh. It is worse on dry, sandy soils. Destroy affected tubers and practise crop rotation.

Viruses cause the leaves to curl up or become mottled or crinkled. The plants are stunted though the tubers are not affected. Viruses are spread by aphids or are present on the seed potatoes.

🌱 Always buy certified seed potatoes and spray aphids with pyrethrum or soft soap if they appear.

SOWING AND GROWING

January–February	Unpack seed potatoes straight away and start them into growth. Lay the tubers out in trays, with the 'rose' end – the one with the greatest concentration of eyes – uppermost. Place the trays in a cool, dry place with good light but not direct sunlight. After a few weeks, sprouts will start to grow. This process, known as chitting, helps to start the tubers into growth and gains a few precious weeks while the soil is too cold for them to grow outdoors. Rub off all but the four strongest sprouts at the rose end.
March	Plant early varieties in milder areas, but wait until early April in colder areas.
April	Plant earlies in colder areas and follow with second earlies and maincrops by the end of the month. Scatter a little balanced fertiliser over the area. Plant tubers about 15cm deep and about 40cm apart. Allow 75cm between rows of maincrops and 45cm between rows of early varieties.
June–July	Watch for the first symptoms of blight and aphids, which can infect the plants with virus (see above). Dig early varieties followed by second earlies from July onwards.
September–October	Lift maincrop potatoes. Delaying beyond this time gives the slugs a chance to damage them, and the weather may deteriorate. Choose a day when the soil is fairly dry.

CARROTS

Forget the giant roots favoured by allotment gardeners and think sweet, crunchy, baby carrots – and you will appreciate how carrots are a perfect crop for the smallest garden. Their fresh, green, feathery foliage makes carrots a good foil for flowers whether in a border or a container. However you grow them, the taste of fresh carrots is incomparable with the supermarket offerings.

In a small garden, in flower borders or in containers try several sowings of a quick-maturing early variety. Maincrop varieties are better on a vegetable plot if you want a single crop for storing over winter.

Preparing and caring

Carrots do best in a deep but well-drained soil. For good crops on a heavy soil it is worth digging the soil over with a garden fork to open it up, especially if the ground is compacted. Do not add any organic matter as this can cause the roots to divide. Break the soil surface down to a crumbly texture with the back of the garden fork and then use a garden rake to get a level seedbed.

On sandy soils, if a hard surface crust has built up, break this up by raking into a fine seedbed. On a typical garden soil, carrots will grow well without additional fertiliser.

Grow carrots in blocks of several short rows rather than one long row, to make it easier to protect them from carrot fly (see page 204) with a barrier. Here are some suggestions for creating suitable barriers:

🌱 Fix a stout post at each corner of the block of carrots, then wrap thick-gauge, transparent plastic sheeting round them to form a wall at least 75cm high. Bury the bottom of the plastic and secure it to the posts, by stapling for example. Make sure the structure will stand up to wind if your garden is exposed.

🌱 Insert hoops over the width of the carrot bed and drape fine plastic netting or fleece over the top. Provided this is well anchored at the edges with bricks or stones, it should prevent small insects getting in but allows light, air and rain to reach the crop.

Carrots do not need watering once they are established unless it is exceptionally dry, so save valuable water for more sensitive crops. Carrots in pots, however, will need regular watering.

Carrot fly is the bane of carrot growers. Tell-tale signs are reddening or yellowing of the foliage and, in severe cases, individual plants may wilt and die, due to carrot fly grubs eating the side roots. Later in the summer, a second generation of grubs starts to burrow into the main tap root. Carrots planted among flowers and in containers should be harder for the pests to find. Try:
– using physical barriers (see page 203)
– sowing seeds after late May or dig them up before early August to miss the main attacks
– growing resistant varieties. Early varieties pulled young are also less likely to suffer than maincrops left in the ground until autumn.

Harvesting and storing

The roots should slide easily out of moist soil when the base of the leaves is pulled gently. If not, use a hand fork to ease the roots out. Pull baby carrots in bunches as required, taking care not to disturb the remaining roots. Leave maincrop carrots in the ground until required over winter. If carrot fly is a problem (see left), lift and store indoors.

To store carrots, cut the tops off just above the root and layer the carrots in slightly moist sand in wooden boxes. Keep them in a cool shed until required in the kitchen.

SOWING AND GROWING

March	Make the first outdoor sowings on lighter soils and in milder areas. Sow directly into the ground as starting them in pots may cause the roots to fork. For a continuous supply of baby carrots, sow a short row or two and keep sowing at regular intervals through the summer. Draw out a shallow 1.5cm seed drill. Space adjacent drills 15cm apart. If the soil is very dry, dribble water into the drill and let this soak in. Aim for a seed every 2.5cm or so to avoid having to thin the young plants later. Cover the drill with dry soil, but to avoid disturbing the seeds, do not water. In a border: sow in patches just as you would hardy annuals. This will make it easier to distinguish carrot seedlings from weeds later on. In containers: scatter the seed thinly – aim for a seed roughly every 2.5cm on moist, weed-free compost. Cover with a further 1.5cm layer of compost.
April	Make the first outdoor sowings on heavier soils. Carrot seed may fail in cold, wet soil, so be prepared to re-sow if this happens.
May	As soon as the seedlings are big enough to handle, gently pull out excess to leave a plant every 2.5cm. If they are too crowded, individual roots may be smaller, but they will push each other apart as they grow. Restrict thinning to a minimum and, if possible, thin in the evening to reduce the risk of attracting carrot fly. Sow maincrop varieties later this month. You need make only one sowing if you store the roots over winter.
June	The first baby carrots should be ready for pulling.
July–August	Keep sowing short rows of an early variety for a continuing supply of baby carrots. And keep pulling earlier sowings before they get too large. If you cannot keep up with picking them, leave them in the ground and dig them up in the autumn. Thin out maincrop varieties to leave 5–7.5cm between plants, to encourage good-sized roots.
September	Harvest maincrop carrots, if carrot fly and slugs are starting to attack them. Otherwise, leave unaffected carrots in the ground until needed. Mark the position of the rows. In very cold areas, cover with a layer of straw or dry bracken to stop the soil from freezing solid.
October	A greenhouse with soil borders is the ideal place for a catch crop of early carrots. Sow after the tomatoes have finished and again in the early spring before the next crop.

Root Crops

GOOD VARIETIES

'Alto' (long, for slicing)

'Boltardy' (reliable older variety)

'Chioggia' (unusual candy striped)

'Pablo' (for baby beets)

BEETROOT

In a small garden, beetroot offers variety, diversity and colour. There are varieties with white, yellow and striped roots, round roots for baby beet and long roots that are easy to slice. Beetroot is ideal for mini-vegetable beds, grows well in containers, and the leaves can be decorative enough for the flower border.

Young beetroot leaves can be used raw in salads and the older leaves can be cooked as spinach. However, if you don't like the roots, you would be better off growing chard, a close relative of beetroot that produces fleshy edible leaf stalks rather than roots (see pages 108–10).

Preparing and caring

Beetroot seeds contain a chemical that inhibits germination until it is washed out by rain after sowing. To give your plants a quick start, try soaking the seed clusters in warm water overnight before sowing. This will also give more even germination.

Beetroot is a surprisingly greedy feeder, so grow it on soil that has been well manured over the years. Alternatively, just before sowing the seeds in the spring, work in a general fertiliser, such as growmore, pelleted chicken manure or blood, fish and bone.

HEALTH WATCH!

Beetroot is generally pretty trouble-free, and any leaf problems should not affect the yield of roots. You may come across:

Leaf miner Tiny grubs burrow in the leaf, causing transparent patches. Pick off badly affected leaves.

Leaf spot Brown, roughly circular spots develop on the leaves and sometimes the centres drop out, giving a 'shot-hole' effect (see page 105).

Root Crops

Multi-seeding is a technique that works well with a number of root vegetables. The idea is that you grow six to eight seedlings in a small pot and plant the whole clump out together. As the plants grow, the roots will push each other apart to produce a clump of small but perfectly round roots. Beetroot is the ideal vegetable for multi-seeding because each of the large corky seed capsules contains up to four seeds.

- Sow two seed clusters in a 7cm pot, 1.5cm deep. Keep the pots somewhere cool but frost-free. Beetroot germinates at temperatures as low as 7°C. Keep the compost moist.
- When the clump of seedlings has developed the first 'true' leaves (the first pair of leaves are actually part of the seed) you can plant it out.
- Dig a hole with a trowel and carefully tap the rootball out of the pot. Plant clumps level with the soil surface, 15cm apart each way.

Do not water beetroot unless the soil is likely to dry out completely. Over-watering will simply produce more leaves rather than roots. Watering or even heavy rain after a very dry spell will cause the roots to split. Water beetroot in pots regularly.

If you prefer to leave your beetroot in the ground for winter use, cover them with straw or soil to prevent them freezing.

Harvesting and storing
For baby beets, pull the roots before they reach golf-ball size. Take care not to disturb any immature plants growing nearby. Try not to break the thin tap root, or the beetroot will bleed. For the same reason, do not cut the foliage off. Twist the leaves off about 2.5–5cm above the root to limit bleeding.

To store maincrop beetroot, place a layer of barely-moist sand in a wooden box. Inspect the roots carefully and reject any damaged ones. Lay them on the sand so that they are not touching. Cover completely with sand and start another layer, and so on until the box is full. Keep the box in a cool, dry but frost-free place. Rinse off soil and remove the skins after cooking.

SOWING AND GROWING

February	Make the earliest sowings under cloches (see page 64).
March–April	Make a seed drill 1.5cm deep. Sow a short row and repeat at fortnightly intervals for a continuous supply of tender baby beet. If early sowings are allowed to become too large, the beetroot will be woody and lose their flavour. Space rows about 15cm apart. If the soil is dry, dribble water into the drill and leave it to soak in. Place a seed every 2.5cm or so along the drill. Cover with soil and water in dry spells until the seedlings emerge. In containers: aim for a seed every 5cm each way. Cover with a 1.5cm layer of compost. In a border: sow directly, as you would hardy annuals. Work in plenty of fertiliser first. In milder areas make the first outdoor sowing in March, but continue using cloches in colder areas. By April it should be safe to sow directly outdoors in all parts of the UK.
May–June	This is the best time to sow for a main crop for harvesting from August or September onwards. Sow as above, pull every other root as a baby beet and leave the remainder to grow on for winter storage. Continue sowing short rows for a regular supply of baby beets. The first sowings are ready to harvest as baby beet.
July	Make a final sowing for baby beets.
October–November	Lift maincrop beetroots for storing indoors. Roots can be left in the ground, but remember that they may be attacked by soil pests, and since some of the roots project above the soil, they can be damaged by severe frosts.

'Gladiator' (reliable older variety)

'Lancer' (slim, baby parsnips)

PARSNIPS

Once thought of as just a winter standby, parsnips are now available from summer onwards as a baby vegetable. In a small garden or even in containers it is possible to grow a quick crop of small parsnips. With more space, parsnip is an easy winter crop – you simply leave it in the ground until you want it.

Parsnips do best on deeply dug, fertile soil with a pH of about 6.5 (just on the acid side). Ideally they should follow a previous crop that has been well-manured rather than have the manure added now. Fork in a small amount of a general fertiliser. Long-rooted types hate stony, heavy or compacted soil, so try a shorter-rooted variety.

Preparing and caring

Parsnip seed loses its viability rapidly. Always buy fresh seed each year – do not save surplus seed. Once the packet has been opened, re-seal it and store it in a cool, dry place if you intend to make further sowings of, for example, baby parsnips.

As they are slow growing, parsnips cannot compete with weeds early in the season. So hoe between the rows regularly in order to keep weeds under control.

Regular water isn't needed for parsnips growing in the ground, but make sure that the soil does not dry out in very hot weather. If necessary, water to re-moisten the soil to a good depth. Heavy watering or rain following a drought, however, will cause the roots to split. Baby parsnips in beds and pots will need watering.

In very cold areas, cover the row with straw to stop the ground freezing solid.

HEALTH WATCH!

Parsnips are sometimes attacked by **carrot fly** (see page 204). To combat this, grow parsnips with carrots and surround both crops with a carrot fly barrier (see page 203) or cover with garden fleece.

parsnips

Root Crops

Harvesting and storing

The flavour of the roots is likely to be better if they are left in the ground until needed. Although frost is said to enhance the flavour, you can lift them before the first frosts if you wish. However, once the ground has frozen they are hard to harvest, so you may prefer to lift them beforehand and store the roots indoors in boxes of sand. Use a garden fork to ease the roots out of the ground.

Aim to finish digging up the parsnips by late winter, before they start to re-grow. Parsnips, like carrots, are biennials and will throw up flowering shoots in the spring.

SOWING AND GROWING

March	Postpone sowing until April unless the site is particularly favourable. Parsnips need a deep, well-worked soil. Sow the seed directly into the ground – starting the seed off in pots usually results in forked roots. Parsnip seed is slow and erratic to germinate, so there is no real advantage in starting too soon.
April	Sow into seed drills 1cm deep and 30cm apart. Sow a couple of seeds at 15cm intervals, to limit the amount of thinning later. If more than one plant comes up at each position, thin out all but the strongest. The seedlings are slow to appear, so sow a quick-growing crop such as radish in the same drill, as a marker. The radishes will be out of the way before the parsnips need the space. For baby parsnips, space the rows 15cm apart and aim for one plant every 5cm.
May–June	Further sowings can be made through the summer for a succession of baby parsnips. Water well until the young plants are established.
July–August	Harvest when the top of the root is between 2.5cm and 5cm wide. Use a hand fork to ease them out.
September	Continue to harvest baby parsnips. The largest roots of winter parsnips can also be lifted before the tops have died off.
October	Once the tops have died down, the roots can be lifted for storing under cover. They can also be left where they are and will keep in good condition until spring.

RESOURCES

Vegetable Calendar

JANUARY

CONTINUE HARVESTING Sprouting broccoli, brussels sprouts, winter cabbages, kale, leeks, parsnips, swedes, winter turnips.

OTHER JOBS Buy vegetable seed, start to chit seed potatoes. Plan where to put your crops. Complete the greenhouse clean-up.

FEBRUARY

SOW FROM SEED INDOORS Beetroot, broad beans, summer cabbages, calabrese, summer cauliflower, lettuces and onions. In milder areas sow outdoors under cloches early beetroot, carrots, lettuces, spring onions, peas, radishes, salad leaf, spinach, early turnips.

CONTINUE HARVESTING Sprouting broccoli, brussels sprouts, kale, leeks, parsnips, swedes, winter turnips.

FINISH HARVESTING Winter cabbages.

OTHER JOBS Feed overwintered greens with nitrogen fertiliser; continue to chit potatoes. Put cloches in position to warm soil. Erect pea and bean supports to save time later; erect a carrot fly barrier.

MARCH

SOW IN POTS INDOORS, IF NOT DONE LAST MONTH Summer cabbages, summer cauliflower, calabrese, celery and celeriac, leeks, lettuces, onions. Also sow aubergines, peppers and tomatoes for greenhouse or for outdoors in milder areas.

MAKE FIRST SOWING OUTDOORS (under cloches in colder areas) of early carrots, spring onions, peas, radishes, salad leaves, spinach and leaf beet, turnips if not done last month.

PLANT Garlic, onion sets, shallots, early potatoes if soil is workable.

START HARVESTING Spring cabbages.

CONTINUE HARVESTING Sprouting broccoli, kale, leeks, parsnips.

FINISH HARVESTING Brussels sprouts, swedes, winter turnips.

PESTS AND DISEASES Watch for slug damage, protect vulnerable plants.

OTHER JOBS Complete winter digging on lighter soils. Apply loose mulches; cover soil with black plastic to plant through later.

APRIL

SOW Celery and celeriac, kale. In milder areas sow French beans and sweetcorn indoors. Outdoors sow broad beans, kohl rabi, leeks, parsnips. Sow aubergine, peppers and outdoor tomatoes if not done already.

PLANT All hardy vegetables sown indoors as soon as weather is suitable; garlic, onion sets and shallots if not done already; maincrop potatoes.

KEEP SOWING Beetroot, calabrese, early carrots, summer cauliflower, lettuces, spring onion, radishes, peas, salad leaves, spinach, turnips.

START HARVESTING Winter cauliflower.

CONTINUE HARVESTING Sprouting broccoli, spring cabbages.

FINISH HARVESTING Kale, leeks, parsnips.

PESTS AND DISEASES Protect vulnerable plants from slugs and snails, flea beetle.

OTHER JOBS Cover summer brassicas and carrots with crop covers to stop flying pests. Remove cloches from early crops – use instead to protect tender crops. Complete soil preparation as winter crops are cleared. Hoe to remove annual weeds.

Vegetable Calendar

MAY

SOW Brussels sprouts, sprouting broccoli, winter cabbages, autumn and winter cauliflower and kale in pots or seedbed. Sow maincrop beetroot and carrots, winter turnips and swedes outdoors; courgettes, outdoor cucumbers, marrows, squash indoors and sweetcorn outdoors in milder areas, or in pots in colder areas.

PLANT Vegetables started in pots last month, including celery, and greenhouse tomatoes in mild areas.

KEEP SOWING Calabrese, carrots, summer cauliflower, fennel, dwarf beans, kohl rabi, lettuces, spring onions, baby parsnips, peas, radishes, salad leaves, spinach, turnips.

START HARVESTING Beetroot, kohl rabi, lettuces, summer radishes, salad leaves, true spinach, turnips.

FINISH HARVESTING Sprouting broccoli, spring cabbages, winter cauliflower.

PESTS AND DISEASES Protect vulnerable plants from slugs and snails during damp spells, and flea beetle. Watch out for pea moth, pea aphid and blackfly.

OTHER JOBS Cover potatoes and other vulnerable crops if frost is predicted.

JUNE

SOW Oriental greens, winter radishes, fennel, maincrop beetroot, turnips and swedes if not done.

PLANT Brussels sprouts, sprouting broccoli, winter cabbages, celery, autumn and winter cauliflower; leeks (if room); courgettes, marrows, squash, outdoor cucumbers, French beans, sweetcorn, outdoor tomatoes.

KEEP SOWING Maincrop beetroot, calabrese, early carrots, summer cauliflower, dwarf beans, kohl rabi, lettuces, spring onions, baby parsnips, radishes, salad leaves, turnips. Start harvesting Broad beans, early carrots, garlic, overwintering sets of onions, salad onions, early potatoes.

CONTINUE HARVESTING Beetroot, kohl rabi, lettuces, summer radishes, salad leaves, spinach, turnips.

PESTS AND DISEASES Asparagus beetle, potato blight – spray as a precaution. Pinch out tips of broad bean plants to reduce blackfly damage.

OTHER JOBS Hoe between rows of seedlings to get rid of annual weeds.

JULY

SOW Spring cabbage in north or in cold areas, oriental greens, winter radish, baby beets.

PLANT Brussels sprouts, sprouting broccoli, winter cauliflower, kale, leeks, oriental greens (if not done last month).

KEEP SOWING Beetroot, calabrese, carrots, summer cauliflower, fennel, kohl rabi, lettuces, spring onions, radishes, baby parsnips, leaf beet, salad leaves, spinach, turnips.

START HARVESTING Summer/autumn cabbages, calabrese, summer/autumn cauliflower, chard, courgettes, endive, French beans, peas, maincrop potatoes, shallots, leaf beet.

CONTINUE HARVESTING Beetroot, early carrots, kohl rabi, lettuce, peas, summer radishes, salad leaves, spinach, turnips.

FINISH HARVESTING Broad beans, garlic, onions from overwintering sets, early potatoes.

PESTS AND DISEASES Look out for blackfly on beans; spray if necessary. Keep spraying to protect potatoes and tomatoes from blight.

OTHER JOBS Dry off garlic, shallots and onions and store for winter use.

Vegetable Calendar

AUGUST

SOW Spring cabbage in milder parts, greenhouse lettuces, autumn sown onions, spinach and leaf beet for winter.

PLANT Any vegetables started off earlier in pots can be used to fill gaps in the garden or vegetable plot.

KEEP SOWING Make last sowing of calabrese, carrots, lettuces, spring onions, radishes and keep sowing salad leaves.

START HARVESTING Celery, outdoor cucumbers, kale, marrows, onions from seed, onions from sets, runner beans, swetcorn, outdoor tomatoes.

CONTINUE HARVESTING Beetroot, summer/autumn cabbages, calabrese, early carrots, summer/autumn cauliflower, chard, courgettes, endive, French beans, kohl rabi, lettuces, peas, maincrop potatoes, summer radishes, salad leaves, leaf beet, turnips.

FINISH HARVESTING Shallots, spinach.

PESTS AND DISEASES Cabbage white caterpillars, mealy cabbage aphid, cabbage whitefly – spray if necessary.

OTHER JOBS Pick courgettes and beans before going on holiday to prolong cropping.

SEPTEMBER

SOW Summer cauliflower for overwintering, greenhouse lettuces.

PLANT Spring cabbages, autumn onions from seed.

KEEP SOWING Make last sowing of salad leaves.

START HARVESTING Brussels sprouts, Chinese cabbage, Florence fennel, leeks, pumpkins, squash, swedes, winter turnips.

CONTINUE HARVESTING Summer/autumn cabbages, calabrese, early carrots, summer/autumn cauliflower, celery, chard, courgettes, outdoor cucumbers, French beans, kale, lettuce, marrows, onions from seed, onions from sets, peas, summer radishes, runner beans, salad leaves, leaf beet, sweetcorn, outdoor tomatoes.

FINISH HARVESTING Beetroot, endive, kohl rabi, maincrop potatoes, turnips.

OTHER JOBS Cover lettuce, oriental greens, spinach with cloches in cold areas.

OCTOBER

SOW Broad beans, peas to overwinter.

PLANT Garlic, salad leaves in modular trays, autumn onion sets, spring cabbages in milder areas. Start harvesting parsnips, winter radishes.

CONTINUE HARVESTING Brussels sprouts, summer/autumn cabbages, calabrese, maincrop carrots, summer/autumn cauliflower, Chinese cabbage, kale, leeks, salad leaves, swedes, turnips.

FINISH HARVESTING Early carrots, celery, chard, courgettes, outdoor cucumbers, Florence fennel, French beans, leaf beet, lettuces, marrows, onions from seed, onions from sets, peas, pumpkins, summer radishes, runner beans, squash, sweetcorn, outdoor tomatoes.

OTHER JOBS Start to clear away plant debris. Cut down dead ferns of asparagus and mulch with organic matter.

NOVEMBER

SOW Garlic if not yet done.

START HARVESTING Winter cabbages.

CONTINUE HARVESTING Brussels sprouts, calabrese, maincrop carrots, kale, leeks, parsnips, swedes, winter turnips.

FINISH HARVESTING Summer/autumn cabbages, summer/autumn cauliflower, Chinese cabbage, winter radishes, salad leaves.

PESTS AND DISEASES Protect overwintered cabbage from pigeons and rabbits with netting.

OTHER JOBS Start a bean trench and winter digging. Finish clearing crop remains and compost it.

DECEMBER

START HARVESTING Sprouting broccoli.

CONTINUE HARVESTING Brussels sprouts, winter cabbages, kale, leeks, parsnips, swedes, winter turnips.

FINISH HARVESTING Calabrese, maincrop carrots.

OTHER JOBS Try to complete winter digging on heavy soils. Check pH and if necessary lime acid soil where brassicas will grow.

▶ Index

A

acid soil 27, 28
alkaline soil 22, 27, 151, 162
allium leaf miner 188
allotments 18–20, 35
aphids 14, 39, 41, 43,
60
  greenhouse 131, 136, 139
  leafy vegetables 90, 94,
98, 109, 172
  root vegetables 197, 201
arches 13, 16, 72, 80
artichokes: globe 13, 15, 16,
145–7
  Jerusalem 145, 147
asparagus 13, 15, 16, 23,
116–17
asparagus beetle 116
aubergine 10, 12, 22, 61,
138–40

B

baby vegetables 10, 17, 108,
158, 166, 206, 210
bark chips 45
bean seed beetle 83
bean seed fly 83
beans 11, 51
  dried 76, 78
  see also specific types
beetroot 10, 12, 13, 16, 23,
206–9
  baby 17, 208
  catch crops 52
  watering 47
bindweed 36, 38
biological controls 41, 43, 60,
112, 113
birds 39, 154–5, 162, 164,
170, 173, 184
black sooty mould 41, 83
blackfly 41, 62, 74, 78, 83
blackleg 200

blight 22, 23, 41, 130, 133,
197, 200
blossom end rot 131, 136,
139
bolting 13, 89, 94, 96, 102,
106, 108, 159, 186
bonemeal 45
Bordeaux mixture 43
borders 13–16, 37, 64,82, 88,
89, 113
boron deficiency 142
bought plants 61–2
brassicas, see cabbage
family
broad beans 12, 15, 16, 22,
82–5
  diseases/pests 51, 70
  dwarf 82, 83
broccoli 22, 166
  sprouting 52, 55, 169–71
Brussels sprouts 12, 22, 52,
55, 162–5

C

cabbage 16, 47, 55, 61,
150–7
  baby vegetables 17
  crop rotation 22
  diseases 156–7
  pests 153–5
  see also specific types
cabbage family 22, 45, 48,
52, 62, 148–78
cabbage root fly 98, 101, 153,
164, 176
cabbage whites 14, 39, 98,
153, 161, 167, 172
calabrese 17, 22, 51, 52, 62,
166–8
calcium 90
carrot fly 39, 105, 204, 211
carrots 10, 12, 13, 16, 23, 55,
202–5

baby 17, 202
  catch crops 52
  frost protection 65
  sowing outdoors 53
catch crops 52, 178
caterpillars 43, 160, 161, 167,
170
cauliflower 12, 22, 51, 52, 55,
62, 158–61
  baby 17, 158, 159
celeriac 23, 104–7
celery 12, 23, 104–7
celery fly grubs 105
chalky soil 28, 44
chard 10, 12, 16, 23, 108–10,
206
chervil 92
chickweed 37, 38
chillies 12, 16, 135–7
Chinese cabbage 96–7, 98,
99
chives 13, 22
chocolate spot 84, 85
chop suey greens 97
clay soil 26, 28, 34, 151,
158
climbers 14, 16
  beans 73–5, 80–1
  peas 68–71
cloches 28, 51, 53, 64,
90
clubroot 22, 41, 62, 98,
101, 156, 162,
164, 170
coldframes 56, 63, 64, 65
colour 10, 13, 88, 150
compost 11, 29–31
  bins 29–30, 31
containers 10–12, 16
  feeding 46
  pest control 41
  watering 11, 12, 48, 49
coriander 92–3

couch grass 38
courgettes 12, 14, 16, 23, 51, 52, 120–4
  baby 17
  buying plants 61, 62
  cloches 65
  diseases/pests 41, 62, 122
  mulching 37, 48
cress 93
crop rotation 21–3, 42, 43, 59
cucumbers 11, 12, 23, 51, 52, 59, 111–15
  baby vegetables 17
  buying plants 61, 63
  pests 62
cutworms 89

D
damping-off 60
dandelion 38
digging 19, 28, 32–4
  clearing weeds 36
diseases 11, 19
  control 40, 41, 43
  crop rotation 21, 22, 59
  greenhouse 59
  see also under individual vegetables
double cropping 51
double digging 32, 33
downy mildew 89, 109, 157, 183
drought 47, 48, 74
dwarf varieties 17, 51

E
earthing up 197, 198
earthworms 34
edging plants 13, 88
eelworms 200
Epsom salts 45
extending season 65

F
fat hen 38
fennel 16, 104–7
fertiliser 11–12, 22, 44–6
flea beetle 98, 101, 153, 160, 172
fleece 23, 39, 51, 63, 64, 65
follow-on crops 52
free-draining soil 26, 28, 44
French beans 12, 16, 17, 22, 73, 79–81
frost 23, 53, 64–5, 198
fruit fly 142
fungicides 40, 41
funnels 48, 112

G
garden centres 61
garden compost 29–30
garlic 12, 22, 191–3
glyphosate 35, 36
greenback 131
greenfly 39, 41, 62
greenhouse 49, 59–60
  buying plants 63
  cucumbers 59, 111, 113–14
  diseases/pests 43, 59, 60, 89
  sowing seed 56–8
  tomatoes 59–60, 130, 132–2, 134
green manure 85
growing bags 11, 59, 111
guttering, plastic 68

H
hairy bittercress 38
halo blight 74
hanging baskets 10, 68, 130
hardening off 62, 63
haricot beans 76

herbs 92
hoeing 38, 48, 83, 184
hose, leaky 49

I
indoor sowing 56–8
insecticides 40, 132, 41
irrigation systems 49, 60

K
kale 12, 13, 15, 16, 22, 52, 55, 172–4
kohl rabi 175–9

L
leaf beet 23, 92, 108–10
leaf miners 109, 207
leaf mould 30, 31, 45
leaf spot 105, 207
leek moth 188
leek rust 188, 192
leeks 12, 13, 15, 16, 22, 55, 187–9
  baby 17, 187
legumes 66–85
lettuce 12, 13, 16, 23, 55, 88–91
  bolting 13, 89
  buying plants 61, 62
  catch crops 52, 75
  dwarf 17
  frost protection 65
  sowing 57
  watering 47
lime 22, 27, 28, 41, 46, 104, 158, 162
liquid feeds 46
loam 26, 28

M
magnesium 45
mangetout 10, 12, 22, 68, 70, 71

index

Index

manure   31, 42, 45, 85
marrows   16, 23, 51, 61, 62, 120, 124–5
mealy cabbage aphid   154, 170, 172
mice   70, 78, 84, 142
mildew   126
mizuna   97
modular trays   57
mosaic virus   78, 105, 122
mulch   14, 34, 37, 47, 48, 59
    sheet   37, 48, 122, 132
multi-seeding   208
mushroom compost   28, 31
mustards   97

N
nematodes   41, 43
netting   22, 23, 39, 43, 74, 98
nitrogen   12, 14, 27, 30, 44–5, 46, 89, 170
    peas/beans   68, 82
nutrients   21, 44–5, 59, 172

O
onion family   22, 23, 180–93
onions   12, 17, 22, 47, 182–6
    spring/salad   16, 52, 53, 54, 65, 186, 190
organic gardening   32, 35, 42–3, 92
    feeding soil   42, 45, 46
    pest control   40, 41, 43
organic matter   19, 21, 22, 28, 29–31, 42, 45
    mulches   34, 47
oriental greens   10, 16, 22, 96–9
ornamental plants   10, 13, 16, 64, 76, 108, 135, 145

outdoor sowing   53–55
overgrown plot   20, 35
overwintered vegetables   51, 52, 190

P
pak choi   94, 97, 98
parsley   23
parsnips   17, 23, 47, 52, 53, 210–12
paths   34, 37
patios   10, 49, 92
pea/bean weevil   70, 84
pea family   22, 23, 66–85
pea moth   70, 71
peas   12, 16, 22, 68–71
    catch crops   52, 75
    pests   51, 70
    sowing outdoors   54
    supports   69
    see also mangetout
peppers   10, 12, 16, 22, 61, 63, 135–7
perennial vegetables   15, 23
pergolas   13, 16
pests   11, 14, 19, 21, 35
    barriers   39, 41, 43
    bought plants   62
    controlling   39–41
    crop rotation   21, 22–3
    greenhouse   60
    hand-picking   41, 43
    organic gardening   42, 43
    natural predators   41, 42, 43
    pesticides   40, 43
    see also under individual vegetables
pH test   27, 162
phosphates   12, 45, 46
phosphorus   45
pigeons   39, 154–5, 164, 170, 173

planting   13, 62, 89
planting hole   34, 112, 121
pollination   76, 143
    by hand   122
potash   12, 45, 46
potassium   45
potager   13, 64
potato blight   22, 41, 43, 131, 197, 200
potato family   22–3
potatoes   12, 22, 37, 45, 196–201
    containers   199
    early   51, 198, 199
    new   10, 196
    pests and diseases   200–1
pots   10, 12, 28, 57, 59
potting on   58
powdery mildew   113, 122, 157
pricking out   58
propagator   56
pumpkins   16, 23, 125–6
pyrethrum   41, 43, 112

R
rabbits   20, 39, 154
radish   12, 22, 52, 65, 100–3
    pods   100, 102
    sowing   53, 54
raised beds   13, 17, 20, 28, 41, 88, 94
    cloches   64
    preparing soil   32
ring spot   157
rocket   93, 94
root crops   23, 194–212
rotovator   35
runner beans   12, 16, 22, 52, 72–5
    buying plants   62
    dwarf   73
    watering   47, 73
rust   84

S

salad burnet	93
salad crops	86–117
salad leaves	10, 12, 92–5
sandy soil	28, 34, 44, 151
Savoy cabbage	13, 15
scab	197, 200
seaweed extract	46
seed	13
sowing	53–4, 57
seedbed	53, 151
seed drill	54
seedlings	55, 58
shade	12, 14, 16, 48, 72, 176
shallots	12, 22, 51, 182–6
single digging	32, 33
slug pellets	40
slugs and snails	14, 40–1, 43, 146, 172
legumes	72, 78
root vegetables	200
salad crops	90, 94, 98, 105
smut	142
snap peas	68
soft soap	41, 43
soil	26–8
crop rotation	22–3
feeding	42
improving	29–31
preparing	32–4
temperature	53, 65
texture	26
types	28
soil rots	111, 132
sowing	43
in bands	54
indoors	56–8
little and often	51
outdoors	53–5
small seeds	58
soya beans	79
space, using	51–2
spider mites	43, 60, 62, 112, 131, 136, 139
spinach	12, 16, 23, 47, 52, 75, 93, 108–10
spraing	201
spring greens	12, 150, 151, 152, 157
squash	16, 23, 51, 118–27
summer	120–4
winter	120, 125–7
stony soil	28
sun-loving vegetables	128–47
supports	14, 69, 74, 81
swedes	175–9
sweetcorn	16, 23, 37, 51, 61, 62, 141–4

T

terracotta pots	11
thinning out	55
tip burn	90
tomato feed	12, 46, 60, 63, 123, 133
tomatoes	22, 45, 51, 52, 130–4
borders	14, 16
buying plants	61, 63
cherry tomatoes	17
cloches	65
containers	10, 11, 12, 45
greenhouse	59–60, 130, 131–2, 134
transplanting	55
trellis	68, 72, 80, 113
trenching	34
tubs	10, 12, 16
turnips	175–9

V

vegetable plot	23
small	17, 22–3, 51, 90
starting off	32

vermiculite	57
vine weevil	11, 43
viruses	41, 62, 201

W

water shortages	50
watercress	93
watering	21, 47–50
containers	11, 12, 48
greenhouse	60
reducing	47–8
runner beans	73
squash	121
watering can	48
waterlogged soil	26, 28
weedkiller	35, 36
weeds	19, 20, 32, 35–8
annual	37
clearing	35–6
control	37–8
perennial	35–6
top five	38
whitefly	43, 60, 113, 131, 139, 155, 170
white rot	183
wigwams	13, 68, 72, 74, 80, 113
wildlife	42, 142
wind	72
window boxes	10, 88, 90, 92, 130
winter radish	100, 102–3
winter squash	125–6
wood chips	45

index

▶ Credits

ABOUT THE CONSULTANT EDITORS STEVE MERCER AND CERI THOMAS

Steve Mercer has worked for *Which? Gardening* since its very beginning,
30 years ago. During that time he has run most of the vegetable trials and
written articles on all aspects of vegetable growing.

Ceri Thomas is Editor of *Which? Gardening*. She studied horticulture at the
University of Reading and RHS Wisley, and is a passionate gardener.